TOP 100 HYMNS
songbook

www.brentwoodbenson.com

© MMX Brentwood-Benson Music Publishing, 2555 Meridian Blvd., Suite 100, Franklin, TN 37067. All Rights Reserved. Unauthorized Duplication Prohibited.

A Mighty Fortress Is Our God

Words and Music by
MARTIN LUTHER
translated by
FREDERICK H. HEDGE

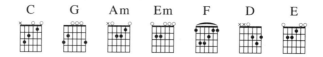

Verse 1

   C G Am G Em C F G C
A mighty fortress is our God, A bulwark never fail- ing;
   C G Am G Em C F G C
Our helper He, amid the flood Of mortal ills prevail- ing:
   C   G D G   F   Am
For still our an- cient foe Doth seek to work us woe;
  Am   G   F   E
His craft and power are great, And, armed with cruel hate,
Am **Em** **C**   **F** **G** **C**
On earth is not his e- qual.

Verse 2

    C G   Am   G
Did we in our own strength confide,
  Em   **C**   **F** **G** **C**
Our striving would be los- ing;
    C   G   Am G
Were not the right Man on our side,
  Em   **C**   **F** **G** **C**
The Man of God's own choos- ing:
    C   G D G   F Am
Dost ask who that may be? Christ Jesus, it is He;
  Am   G   F   E
Lord Sabaoth, His name, From age to age the same,
Am **Em**   **C**   **F** **G** **C**
And He must win the bat- tle.

Arr. © Copyright 2010 Universal Music - Brentwood-Benson Publishing (ASCAP)
(Licensing through Music Services). All rights reserved. Used by permission.

Verse 3

     C   **G**   **Am G**
And though this world, with devils filled,
    Em **C** **F G C**
Should threaten to undo us,
    C   **G**   **Am** **G**
We will not fear, for God hath willed
    Em **C** **F G C**
His truth to triumph through us:
    C   **G D G**   **F** **Am**
The prince of darkness grim, We tremble not for him;
    Am   **G** **F**   **E**
His rage we can endure, For lo, his doom is sure:
Am Em C   **F G C**
One little word shall fell him.

Verse 4

     C   **G**   **Am** **G**
That word above all earthly powers,
    Em **C** **F G C**
No thanks to them, abid- eth;
    C   **G**   **Am** **G**
The Spirit and the gifts are ours
      Em **C** **F G C**
Through Him who with us sid- eth.
    C   **G D G**   **F** **Am**
Let goods and kin- dred go, This mortal life also;
    Am   **G** **F**   **E**
The body they may kill; God's truth abideth still:
Am Em **C** **F G C**
His kingdom is forev- er.

Abide with Me

Words by HENRY FRANCIS LYTE
Music by WILLIAM HENRY MONK

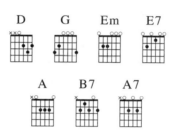

Verse 1
    D   G   D
Abide with me: fast falls the eventide;
D   **G D Em**   **E7 A**
The darkness deepens; Lord, with me abide:
D   **G**   **B7**   **Em**
When other helpers fail, and comforts flee,
A7   **D**   **G D A D**
Help of the helpless, O abide with me!

Verse 2
    D   **G**   **D**
Swift to its close ebbs out life's little day;
D   **G D Em**   **E7 A**
Earth's joys grow dim, its glories pass away;
D   **G B7**   **Em**
Change and decay in all around I see:
A7   **D**   **G D A D**
O Thou who changest not, abide with me!

Arr. © Copyright 2010 Universal Music - Brentwood-Benson Publishing (ASCAP)
(Licensing through Music Services). All rights reserved. Used by permission.

Verse 3

```
           D                  G           D
           I need Thy presence every passing hour;
           D         G    D  Em     E7     A
           What but Thy grace can  foil the tempter's power?
           D                  G        B7     Em
           Who like Thyself my guide and stay can be?
           A7              D       G  D  A  D
           Through cloud and sunshine, O  abide with me!
```

Verse 4

```
           D                    G           D
           Hold Thou Thy cross before my closing eyes;
           D            G    D  Em     E7     A
           Shine through the gloom, and  point me to the skies:
           D                  G        B7     Em
           Heaven's morning breaks and earth's vain shadows flee:
           A7       D      G   D   A   D
           In life, in death, O Lord, abide with me!
```

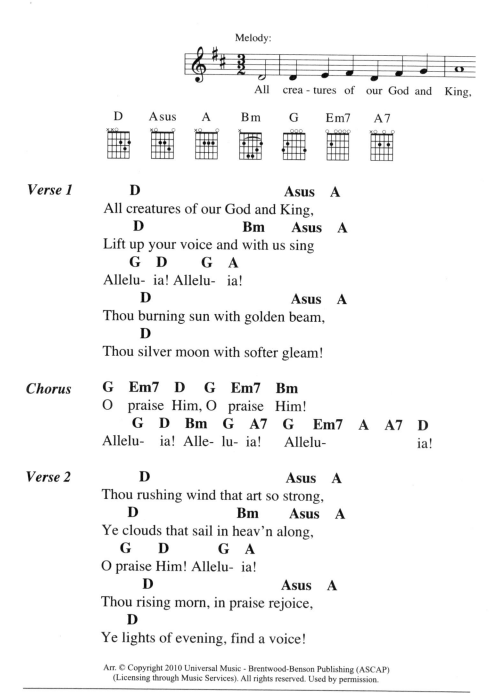

Verse 3
        D   Asus A
And all ye men of tender heart,
       D   Bm   Asus A
Forgiving others, take your part,
  G   D   G   A
O sing ye! Allelu- ia!
       D   Asus A
Ye who long pain and sorrow bear,
       D
Praise God and on Him cast your care!

Verse 4
       D   Asus A
Let all things their Creator bless,
       D   Bm   Asus A
And worship Him in humbleness,
  G   D   G   A
O praise Him! Allelu- ia!
       D   Asus A
Praise, praise the Father, praise the Son,
       D
And praise the Spirit, Three in One!

Verse 5
       D   Asus A
Praise God, from whom all blessings flow;
       D   Bm   Asus A
Praise Him, all creatures here below;
  G   D   G   A
O praise Him! Allelu- ia!
       D   Asus A
Praise Him above, ye heavenly host;
       D
Praise Father, Son, and Holy Ghost.

All Hail the Power of Jesus' Name!

Words by EDWARD PERRONET
Music by OLIVER HOLDEN

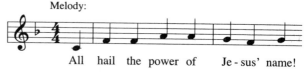

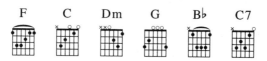

Verse 1
      F   C
All hail the power of Jesus' name!
    C   F   C   F
Let angels prostrate fall;
    F
Bring forth the royal diadem,
        F   C   Dm C G   C
And crown Him Lord of   all;
        F   C
Bring forth the royal diadem,
        F   B♭ F   C7   F
And crown Him Lord   of all.

Verse 2
        F   C
Ye chosen seed of Israel's race,
    C   F   C   F
Ye ransomed from the fall,
    F
Hail Him who saves you by His grace,
        F   C   Dm C G   C
And crown Him Lord of   all;
    F   C
Hail Him who saves you by His grace,
        F   B♭ F   C7   F
And crown Him Lord   of all.

Arr. © Copyright 2010 Universal Music - Brentwood-Benson Publishing (ASCAP)
(Licensing through Music Services). All rights reserved. Used by permission.

Verse 3

      F   C
Let every kindred, every tribe
  C   F   C   F
On this terres- trial ball,
  F
To Him all majesty ascribe,
  F   C   Dm   C   G   C
And crown Him Lord of   all;
  F   C
To Him all majesty ascribe,
  F   B♭ F   C7   F
And crown Him Lord   of all.

Verse 4

      F   C
O that with yonder sacred throng
  C   F   C   F
We at His feet may fall!
      F
We'll join the everlasting song,
  F   C   Dm   C   G   C
And crown Him Lord of   all;
  F   C
We'll join the everlasting song,
  F   B♭ F   C7   F
And crown Him Lord   of all.

Amazing Grace!

Words by JOHN NEWTON
(Stanza 5 by JOHN P. REES)
Music: Traditional American Melody

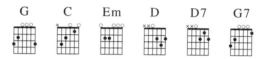

Verse 1
      G   C   G
Amazing grace! how sweet the sound
      G   Em   D D7
That saved a wretch like me!
      G   G7   C   G
I once was lost but now am found,
    Em   D7   G
Was blind, but now I see.

Verse 2
      G   C   G
'Twas grace that taught my heart to fear,
      G   Em   D D7
And grace my fears relieved;
      G   G7   C   G
How precious did that grace appear
    Em   D7   G
The hour I first believed!

Arr. © Copyright 2010 Universal Music - Brentwood-Benson Publishing (ASCAP)
(Licensing through Music Services). All rights reserved. Used by permission.

Verse 3

```
            G              C        G
Through many dangers, toils and snares
     G     Em    D   D7
I have already come;
       G       G7      C      G
'Tis grace hath brought me safe thus far,
      Em       D7      G
And grace will lead me home.
```

Verse 4

```
            G              C     G
The Lord has promised good to me,
       G     Em    D   D7
His word my hope secures;
       G       G7      C     G
He will my shield and portion be
      Em   D7    G
As long as life endures.
```

Verse 5

```
            G                  C       G
When we've been there ten thousand years,
       G      Em    D   D7
Bright shining as the sun,
          G     G7    C         G
We've no less days to sing God's praise
      Em       D7      G
Than when we first begun.
```

And Can It Be

Words by CHARLES WESLEY
Music by THOMAS CAMPBELL

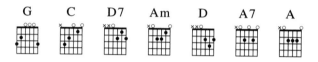

Verse 1
    G   C   D7   G
And can it be that I   should gain
    Am   D   G   D   A7   D
An in-   t'rest in the Sav- ior's blood?
D   G D   G   D
Died He for me,   who caused His pain?
    C   G   D   G
For me, who Him to death pur- sued?
G D   G   C   A   D
A- mazing love! how can it   be
    G   C   D   G
That Thou, my God, should die for me?

Chorus
    G   D   D7   G
Amazing love! how can it be
    C   G   Am G D7 G
That Thou, my God, should die for   me!

Verse 2
```
          G                  C   D7  G
          He left His Father's throne a-  bove,
            Am  D   G    D   A7   D
          So free, so infinite His  grace;
          D          G  D   G        D
          Emptied Himself  of all but love,
               C      G        D   G
          And bled for Adam's helpless race.
          G  D    G       C    A   D
          'Tis mercy all, immense and free;
              G       C     D    G
          O praise my God, it reaches me.
```

Verse 3
```
          G                   C   D7  G
          Long my imprisoned spir- it    lay
            Am   D   G      D   A7   D
          Fast bound in  sin and na- ture's night;
          D          G    D   G         D
          Thine eye diffused   a quickening ray,
              C      G            D   G
          I woke, the dungeon flamed with light.
          G  D      G      C    A   D
          My chains fell off, my heart was free;
              G      C       D     G
          I rose, went forth and followed Thee.
```

Verse 4
```
          G              C    D7  G
          No condemnation now I    dread;
            Am   D   G   D   A7    D
          Jesus, and all in Him is   mine!
          D          G   D    G      D
          Alive in Him,  my living Head,
                C         G          D  G
          And clothed in righteousness di- vine;
          G    D  G       C    A    D
          Bold I approach the eter- nal throne
                G      C            D       G
          And claim the crown, through Christ, my own.
```

Are You Washed in the Blood?

Words and Music by
ELISHA A. HOFFMAN

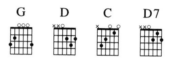

Verse 1
          G
Have you been to Jesus for the cleansing power?
         G   D
Are you washed in the blood of the Lamb?
         G   C
Are you fully trusting in His grace this hour?
         G   D7   G
Are you washed in the blood of the Lamb?

Chorus
         G   C
Are you washed in the blood,
         G   D
In the soul-cleansing blood of the Lamb?
         G   C
Are your garments spotless? Are they white as snow?
         G   D7   G
Are you washed in the blood of the Lamb?

Arr. © Copyright 2010 Universal Music - Brentwood-Benson Publishing (ASCAP)
(Licensing through Music Services). All rights reserved. Used by permission.

Verse 2

        G
Are you walking daily by the Savior's side?
        G   **D**
Are you washed in the blood of the Lamb?
        G   **C**
Do you rest each moment in the Crucified?
        G   **D7**   **G**
Are you washed in the blood of the Lamb?

Verse 3

        G
When the Bridegroom cometh will your robes be white?
        G   **D**
Are you washed in the blood of the Lamb?
        G   **C**
Will your soul be ready for the mansions bright,
        G   **D7**   **G**
And be washed in the blood of the Lamb?

Verse 4

        G
Lay aside the garments that are stained with sin,
        G   **D**
And be washed in the blood of the Lamb;
        G   **C**
There's a fountain flowing for the soul unclean,
        G   **D7**   **G**
O be washed in the blood of the Lamb!

At the Cross

Words by ISAAC WATTS
Music by RALPH E. HUDSON

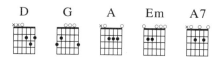

Verse 1
      D
Alas, and did my Savior bleed,
   G   A
And did my Sov'reign die?
      D
Would He devote that sacred head
Em   A7   D
For sinners such as I?

Chorus
      D   A
At the cross, at the cross where I first saw the light,
   A7   D
And the burden of my heart rolled away,
   G   D
It was there by faith I received my sight,
   Em   A7   D
And now I am happy all the day!

Verse 2
      D
Was it for crimes that I had done
  G   **A**
He groaned upon the tree?
  D
Amazing pity, grace unknown,
  Em **A7** **D**
And love beyond degree!

Verse 3
      D
Well might the sun in darkness hide,
  G   **A**
And shut his glories in
  D
When Christ the mighty Maker died
  Em **A7** **D**
For man, the creature's sin.

Verse 4
      D
Thus might I hide my blushing face
  G   **A**
While Calvary's cross appears,
  D
Dissolve my heart in thankfulness,
  Em **A7** **D**
And melt mine eyes to tears.

Verse 5
      D
But drops of grief can ne'er repay
  G   **A**
The debt of love I owe;
  D
Here, Lord, I give myself away,
  Em **A7** **D**
'Tis all that I can do.

Be Thou My Vision

Traditional

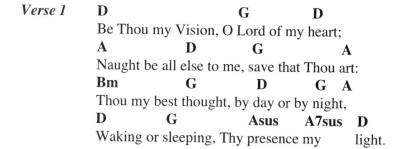

Verse 1
```
D                        G         D
Be Thou my Vision, O Lord of my heart;
A           D          G          A
Naught be all else to me, save that Thou art:
Bm          G          D          G    A
Thou my best thought, by day or by night,
D          G          Asus    A7sus  D
Waking or sleeping, Thy presence my      light.
```

Verse 2
```
D                        G         D
Be Thou my Wisdom, and Thou my true Word;
A           D          G          A
I ever with Thee and Thou with me, Lord:
Bm          G      D          G    A
Thou my great Father, I Thy true son,
D          G          Asus    A7sus  D
Thou in me dwelling, and I with Thee    one.
```

Arr. © Copyright 2010 Universal Music - Brentwood-Benson Publishing (ASCAP)
(Licensing through Music Services). All rights reserved. Used by permission.

Verse 3

D		G	D

Riches I heed not, or man's empty praise,

A	D	G	A

Thou mine inheritance, now and always:

Bm	G	D	G	A

Thou and Thou only, first in my heart,

D	G	Asus	A7sus	D

High King of heaven, my treasure Thou art.

Verse 4

D		G	D

High King of heaven, my victory won,

A	D	G	A

May I reach heaven's joys, O bright heav'n's Sun!

Bm	G	D	G	A

Heart of my own heart, whatever befall,

D	G	Asus	A7sus	D

Still be my Vision, O Ruler of all.

Because He Lives

Words by WILLIAM J. GAITHER
and GLORIA GAITHER
Music by WILLIAM J. GAITHER

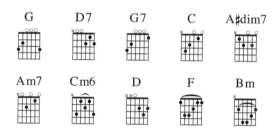

Verse 1   G   D7   G   G7   C
                    God sent His   Son –   they called Him Jesus;
                       G D7 G
                He came to love,
                  G A♯dim7 Am7 D7
                Heal and for-   give.
                    G G7   C
                He lived and died   to buy my pardon;
               C Cm6 G   D7   G
                An empty   grave is there to prove my Savior lives.

© Copyright 1971 William J. Gaither, Inc. (All rights controlled by Gaither Copyright Management).
All rights reserved. Used by permission.

Chorus

      C D7 G G7   C
Because He lives I can face tomorrow;
        G D G   Am7 D7
Because He lives, all fear is gone.
    C D7 G D7 G7 F G7 C
Because I know He holds the future,
    Cm6 G   C G
And life is worth the liv-ing
D7 Bm D7 G
Just because He lives.

Verse 2

G   D7 G G7   C
How sweet to hold a newborn baby,
    G D7 G
And feel the pride
  G A♯dim7 Am7 D7
And joy he gives;
    G G7   C
But greater still the calm assurance:
  C Cm6 G   D7   G
This child can face uncertain days because He lives.

Verse 3

G   D7 G G7   C
And then one day I'll cross the river;
    G D7 G
I'll fight life's fi-   nal
G A♯dim7 Am7 D7
War with pain.
    G G7   C
And then, as death gives way to vict'ry,
  C Cm6 G   D7   G
I'll see the lights of glory and I'll know He reigns.

Blessed Assurance

Words by FANNY J. CROSBY
Music by PHOEBE P. KNAPP

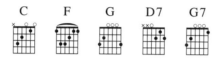

Verse 1
      C   F   C
Blessed assurance, Jesus is mine!
     C   G   D7   G
Oh, what a foretaste of glory divine!
C   F   C
Heir of salvation, purchase of God,
      F   C   G7   C
Born of His Spirit, washed in His   blood.

Chorus
      C   F   C
This is my story, this is my song,
     F   C   D7   G
Praising my Savior   all the day long;
G7   C   F   C
This is my story, this is my song,
     F   C   G7   C
Praising my Savior all the day   long.

Arr. © Copyright 2010 Universal Music - Brentwood-Benson Publishing (ASCAP)
(Licensing through Music Services). All rights reserved. Used by permission.

Verse 2
              C   F   C
Perfect submission, perfect delight,
       C G   D7   G
Visions of rap-ture now burst on my sight:
C   F   C
Angels descending bring from above
         F   C   G7 C
Echoes of mercy, whispers of   love.

Verse 3
              C   F   C
Perfect submission, all is at rest,
      C G   D7   G
I in my Savior am happy and blest;
C   F   C
Watching and waiting, looking above,
         F   C   G7 C
Filled with His goodness, lost in His love.

Breathe on Me, Breath of God

Words by EDWIN HATCH
Music by ROBERT JACKSON

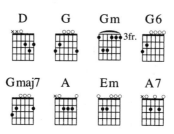

Verse 1
D   G   Gm D
Breathe on me, Breath of   God,
D   G6 Gmaj7 A
Fill me with life   a-   new,
D   Gmaj7 Em
That I may love what Thou dost love,
     D   A7   D
And do what Thou wouldst do.

Verse 2
D   G Gm D
Breathe on me, Breath of   God,
D   G6 Gmaj7 A
Until my heart is   pure,
D   Gmaj7 Em
Until my will is one with Thine,
   D A7 D
To do and to endure.

Arr. © Copyright 2010 Universal Music - Brentwood-Benson Publishing (ASCAP)
(Licensing through Music Services). All rights reserved. Used by permission.

Verse 3
    D   G   Gm   D
Breathe on me, Breath of   God,
    D   G6 Gmaj7 A
Till I am whol- ly   Thine,
    D   Gmaj7 Em
Till all this earthly part of me
        D   A7   D
Glows with Thy fire divine.

Verse 4
    D   G   Gm   D
Breathe on me, Breath of   God,
    D   G6 Gmaj7 A
So shall I nev- er   die,
    D   Gmaj7 Em
But live with Thee the perfect life
        D   A7   D
Of Thine eterni- ty.

Bless the Lord, O My Soul

Traditional

Melody:

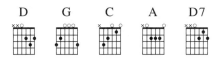

Chorus   **D**   **G**   **C**
Bless the Lord, O my soul;
       A   **D**
Bless the Lord, O my soul;
  G   **C**
And all that is within me
       G **D7** **G**
Bless His ho- ly   name.

Arr. © Copyright 2010 Universal Music - Brentwood-Benson Publishing (ASCAP)
(Licensing through Music Services). All rights reserved. Used by permission.

Christ Arose

Words and Music by
ROBERT LOWRY

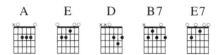

Verse 1
  A   E   A
Low in the grave He lay– Jesus, my Savior!
D   A   B7   E
Waiting the coming day– Jesus, my Lord!

Chorus
A
Up from the grave He arose,
        A   D   A
With a mighty triumph o'er His foes.
E7   A
He arose a victor from the dark domain,
    B7   E
And He lives forever with His saints to reign.
    A   D   A   E7   A
He arose! He arose! Hallelujah! Christ arose!

Verse 2
  A   E   A
Vainly they watch His bed– Jesus, my Savior!
D   A   B7   E
Vainly they seal the dead– Jesus, my Lord!

Verse 3
  A   E   A
Death cannot keep his prey– Jesus, my Savior!
D   A   B7   E
He tore the bars away– Jesus, my Lord!

Arr. © Copyright 2010 Universal Music - Brentwood-Benson Publishing (ASCAP)
(Licensing through Music Services). All rights reserved. Used by permission.

Christ the Lord Is Risen Today

Words by CHARLES WESLEY
Music: *Lyra Davidica (1708)*

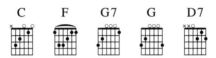

Verse 1
| C | F | C | F | C | G7 | C |

Christ the Lord is risen today, Al- lelu- ia!
F　　　　　　C　　　G　C　F　C　G7　C
Sons of men and angels say, Al- lelu- ia!
G　　　　　　C　　　　　　G　D7　G
Raise your joys and triumphs high, Allelu- ia!
G　　　C　　　　F　　　C　F　C　G7　C
Sing, ye heavens and earth reply, Alle- lu- ia!

Verse 2
C　　　　　　F　　　　C　F　C　G7　C
Lives again our glorious King, Al- lelu- ia!
F　　　　　　C　　　G　C　F　C　G7　C
Where, O Death, is now thy sting? Al- lelu- ia!
G　　　C　　　　　　G　D7　G
Dying once He all doth save, Allelu- ia!
G　　　C　F　　　C　F　C　G7　C
Where thy victory, O Grave? Alle- lu- ia!

Arr. © Copyright 2010 Universal Music - Brentwood-Benson Publishing (ASCAP)
(Licensing through Music Services). All rights reserved. Used by permission.

Verse 3

```
           C                   F            C    F   C  G7   C
           Love's redeeming work is done,   Al-  lelu-     ia!
           F              C         G  C   F   C  G7   C
           Fought the fight, the battle won,   Al-  lelu-   ia!
           G              C              G      D7    G
           Death in vain forbids Him rise, Allelu-    ia!
           G      C     F       C    F   C  G7   C
           Christ hath opened Paradise,  Alle- lu-    ia!
```

Verse 4

```
           C                 F          C    F   C  G7   C
           Soar we now where Christ has led,  Al- lelu-   ia!
           F              C      G  C   F  C  G7   C
           Foll'wing our exalted Head,  Al- lelu-    ia!
           G              C              G      D7    G
           Made like Him, like Him we rise, Allelu-   ia!
           G      C     F           C    F   C  G7   C
           Ours the cross, the grave, the skies, Alle- lu-  ia!
```

Come, Thou Almighty King

Words: Anonymous
Music by FELICE de GIARDINI

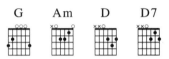

Verse 1
    G   Am   D   G
Come, Thou Almight- y   King,
G   D7 G   D
Help us Thy name to   sing;
G   D
Help us to praise:
D   G   D   G
Father, all-glorious, O'er all victorious,
G   Am   D7 G
Come and reign over us, Ancient of   Days.

Verse 2
    G   Am   D   G
Come, Thou Incar- nate Word,
G   D7 G   D
Gird on Thy might-y   sword;
G   D
Our prayer attend!
D   G   D   G
Come, and Thy people bless, And give Thy word success:
G   Am D7 G
Spirit of holiness, On us de- scend.

Arr. © Copyright 2010 Universal Music - Brentwood-Benson Publishing (ASCAP)
(Licensing through Music Services). All rights reserved. Used by permission.

Verse 3

G	Am	D	G

Come, Holy Com- fort-er,

G	D7	G	D

Thy sacred wit- ness bear

G	D

In this glad hour!

D	G	D	G

Thou, who almighty art, Now rule in every heart

G	Am	D7	G

And ne'er from us depart, Spirit of power.

Verse 4

G	Am	D	G

To Thee great One in Three,

G	D7	G	D

The highest prais-es be,

G	D

Hence evermore;

D	G	D	G

Thy sov'reign majesty May we in glory see,

G	Am	D7	G

And to eternity Love and a- dore.

me, Thou Fount of Every Blessing

Words by ROBERT ROBINSON
Music: American Folk Melody

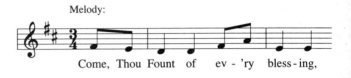

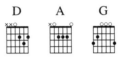

Verse 1

          D   A
Come, Thou Fount of every blessing,
D   G   A   D
Tune my heart to sing Thy grace;
          D   A
Streams of mercy, never ceasing,
D   G   A   D
Call for songs of loudest praise:
          D
Teach me some melodious sonnet,
          D
Sung by flaming tongues above;
          D   A
Praise the mount! I'm fixed upon it,
D   G   A   D
Mount of Thy redeeming love.

Arr. © Copyright 2010 Universal Music - Brentwood-Benson Publishing (ASCAP)
(Licensing through Music Services). All rights reserved. Used by permission.

Verse 2

```
        D              A
Here I raise mine Ebenezer;
D       G       A       D
Hither by Thy help I'm come;
        D                 A
And I hope, by Thy good pleasure,
D       G   A   D
Safely to arrive at home:
            D
Jesus sought me when a stranger,
              D
Wand'ring from the fold of God;
        D               A
He, to rescue me from danger,
D    G       A     D
Interposed His precious blood.
```

Verse 3

```
         D                A
O to grace how great a debtor
D       G       A       D
Daily I'm constrained to be!
           D                  A
Let Thy grace, Lord, like a fetter,
D       G       A       D
Bind my wand'ring heart to Thee:
              D
Prone to wander, Lord, I feel it,
             D
Prone to leave the God I love;
                D                A
Here's my heart, Lord, take and seal it;
D       G       A       D
Seal it for Thy courts above.
```

Count Your Blessings

Words by JOHNSON OATMAN, JR.
Music by EDWIN O. EXCELL

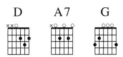

Verse 1   **D**   **A7**
When upon life's billows you are tempest tossed,
A7   **D**
When you are discouraged, thinking all is lost,
D   **A7**
Count your many blessings, name them one by one,
A7   **D**   **A7** **D**
And it will surprise you what the Lord hath done.

Chorus   **D**   **A7**
Count your blessings, name them one by one;
A7   **D**
Count your blessings, see what God hath done;
D   **G**   **A7**   **G**   **A7**
Count your blessings, name them one by one;
D   **G**   **D** **A7** **D**
Count your many blessings, see what God hath done.

Arr. © Copyright 2010 Universal Music - Brentwood-Benson Publishing (ASCAP)
(Licensing through Music Services). All rights reserved. Used by permission.

Verse 2
    D   **A7**
Are you ever burdened with a load of care?
  A7   **D**
Does the cross seem heavy you are called to bear?
 D   **A7**
Count your many blessings, every doubt will fly,
 A7   **D** **A7** **D**
And you will be singing as the days go   by.

Verse 3
    D   **A7**
When you look at others with their lands and gold,
 A7   **D**
Think that Christ has promised you His wealth untold.
 D   **A7**
Count your many blessings, money cannot buy
 A7   **D** **A7** **D**
Your reward in heaven, nor your home on   high.

Verse 4
    D   **A7**
So amid the conflict, whether great or small,
 A7   **D**
Do not be discouraged, God is over all;
 D   **A7**
Count your many blessings, angels will attend,
 A7   **D** **A7** **D**
Help and comfort give you to your journey's end.

Crown Him with Many Crowns

Words by MATTHEW BRIDGES
and GODFREY THRING
Music by GEORGE J. ELVEY

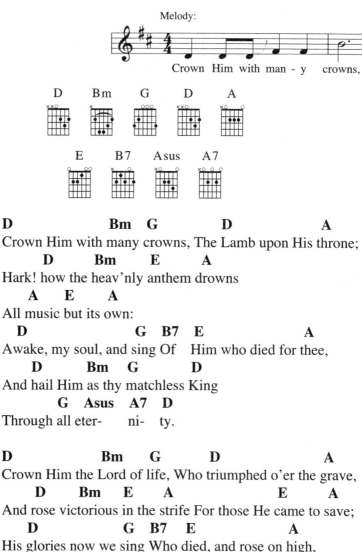

Verse 1
```
        D           Bm  G           D              A
        Crown Him with many crowns, The Lamb upon His throne;
           D      Bm      E        A
        Hark! how the heav'nly anthem drowns
           A    E    A
        All music but its own:
           D              G   B7  E                A
        Awake, my soul, and sing Of  Him who died for thee,
           D      Bm     G       D
        And hail Him as thy matchless King
           G    Asus  A7  D
        Through all eter-  ni-  ty.
```

Verse 2
```
        D           Bm  G        D                    A
        Crown Him the Lord of life, Who triumphed o'er the grave,
           D       Bm    E    A                  E        A
        And rose victorious in the strife For those He came to save;
           D             G   B7  E              A
        His glories now we sing Who died, and rose on high,
           D       Bm    G      D
        Who died eternal  life to bring,
           G     Asus  A7   D
        And lives that death  may  die.
```

Arr. © Copyright 2010 Universal Music - Brentwood-Benson Publishing (ASCAP)
(Licensing through Music Services). All rights reserved. Used by permission.

Verse 3

```
          D           Bm      G           D              A
          Crown Him the Lord of peace, Whose pow'r a scepter sways
             D    Bm        E      A
          From pole to pole, that wars may cease,
             A    E      A
          And all be pray'r and praise:
             D              G   B7    E              A
          His reign shall know no end, And round His pierced feet
             D         Bm    G      D
          Fair flow'rs of para- dise extend
             G          Asus   A7   D
          Their fragrance ev-    er   sweet.
```

Verse 4

```
          D           Bm     G    D             A
          Crown Him the Lord of love; Behold His hands and side,
                D       Bm    E    A         E     A
          Those wounds, yet visi- ble above, In beauty glorified:
                D          G   B7   E              A
          All hail, Redeemer hail! For Thou has died for me:
             D           Bm    G      D
          Thy praise and glory shall not fail
               G     Asus  A7   D
          Throughout eter-  ni-  ty.
```

Down at the Cross

Words by ELISHA A. HOFFMAN
Music by JOHN H. STOCKTON

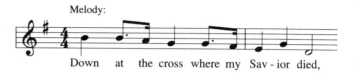

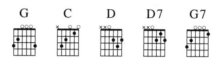

Verse 1
    G   C   G
Down at the cross where my Savior died,
G   D
Down where for cleansing from sin I cried,
G   C   G
There to my heart was the blood applied;
G   D7   G   G7
Glory to His name!

Chorus
    C   G
Glory to His name,
G   D
Glory to His name:
G   C   G
There to my heart was the blood applied;
G   D7   G   G7
Glory to His name!

Arr. © Copyright 2010 Universal Music - Brentwood-Benson Publishing (ASCAP)
(Licensing through Music Services). All rights reserved. Used by permission.

Verse 2
```
         G                  C         G
         I am so wondrously saved from sin,
         G                         D
         Jesus so sweetly abides within;
         G                      C      G
         There at the cross where He took me in;
         G    D7   G    G7
         Glory to His name!
```

Verse 3
```
         G                        C        G
         Oh, precious fountain that saves from sin,
         G                  D
         I am so glad I have entered in;
         G                     C       G
         There Jesus saves me and keeps me clean;
         G    D7   G    G7
         Glory to His name!
```

Verse 4
```
         G                   C     G
         Come to this fountain so rich and sweet,
         G                        D
         Cast thy poor soul at the Savior's feet;
         G                    C      G
         Plunge in today and be made complete;
         G    D7   G    G7
         Glory to His name!
```

Doxology

Words by THOMAS KEN
Music: *OLD 100TH*

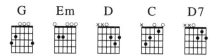

Chorus

        G   Em D G
Praise God, from whom all bless- ings flow;
        G   C   G   D
Praise Him, all creatures here be- low.
    D   G   C   D   G
Praise Him above, ye heavenly host;
    G   D7   G   D G
Praise Father, Son, and Ho- ly   Ghost.
C G
A- men.

Father, I Adore You

Words and Music by
TERRYE COELHO STROM

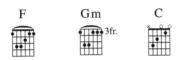

Verse 1
    F Gm   C   F   Gm   C   F
    Fa- ther, I adore You; Lay my life before You;
    Gm   C   F
    How I   love You.

Verse 2
    F Gm   C   F   Gm   C   F
    Je- sus, I adore You; Lay my life before You;
    Gm   C   F
    How I   love You.

Verse 3
    F Gm   C   F   Gm   C   F
    Spirit, I adore You; Lay my life before You;
    Gm   C   F
    How I   love You.

© Copyright 1972 Maranatha Music / CCCM Music (ASCAP) (Both administered by Music Services).
All rights reserved. Used by permission.

Fairest Lord Jesus

Traditional

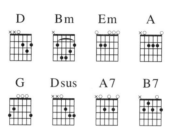

Verse 1
    D Bm   Em   A   D   Bm   Em   A   D
Fairest Lord Je-   sus, Ruler of all na-   ture,
    D   G   D   Dsus   D   A7   D   A
O   Thou of God and   man the Son;
    D   G   B7   Em   B7   Em   A7   D
Thee will I cher- ish, Thee will I   hon- or,
    Bm   G   D   A7   D
Thou, my soul's glory, joy, and crown.

Verse 2
    D Bm   Em   A   D   Bm   Em   A   D
Fair are the mead-   ows, Fairer still the wood-   lands,
    D   G   D   Dsus   D   A7   D   A
Robed in the blooming   garb of   spring;
    D   G   B7   Em   B7   Em   A7   D
Je- sus is fair- er, Jesus   is   pur- er,
    Bm   G   D   A7   D
Who makes the woeful heart to sing.

Arr. © Copyright 2010 Universal Music - Brentwood-Benson Publishing (ASCAP)
(Licensing through Music Services). All rights reserved. Used by permission.

Verse 3

D	Bm	Em	A	D		Bm	Em	A	D

Fair is the sun- shine, Fairer still the moon- light

D G   D   Dsus D A7 D   A

And all the twinkling,   star- ry host;

D G   B7 Em   B7 Em A7   D

Je- sus shines brighter, Jesus shines pur- er

Bm   G   D   A7   D

Than all the angels heav'n can boast.

Verse 4

D Bm Em A D   Bm Em A   D

Beautiful Sav- ior, Lord of all the na- tions,

D G   D Dsus D A7 D   A

Son of God and   Son of man!

D G   B7 Em   B7 Em A7   D

Glory and hon- or, Praise, ad- o- ra- tion,

Bm   G   D   A7   D

Now and forevermore be Thine!

God Will Take Care of You

Words by CIVILLA D. MARTIN
Music by W. STILLMAN MARTIN

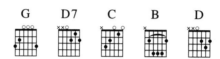

Verse 1 **G**
Be not dismayed whate'er betide,
D7   **G**
God will take care of you;
G
Beneath His wings of love abide,
D7   **G**
God will take care of you.

Chorus **C**   **G**
God will take care of you,
G   **D7**   **G**
Through every day, o'er all the way;
G   **C**   **B**
He will take care of you,
C   **G D G**
God will take care of you.

Arr. © Copyright 2010 Universal Music - Brentwood-Benson Publishing (ASCAP)
(Licensing through Music Services). All rights reserved. Used by permission.

Verse 2   **G**
Through days of toil when heart doth fail,
D7   **G**
God will take care of you;
G
When dangers fierce your path assail,
D7   **G**
God will take care of you.

Verse 3   **G**
No matter what may be the test,
D7   **G**
God will take care of you;
G
Lean, weary one, upon His breast,
D7   **G**
God will take care of you.

Grace Greater than Our Sin

Words by JULIA JOHNSTON
Music by DANIEL TOWNER

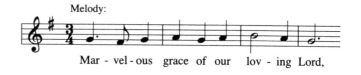

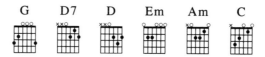

Verse 1   G   D7   G   D7 G
Marvelous grace of our lov- ing   Lord,
D   G
Grace that exceeds our sin and our guilt,
G   D7   G   D7   Em
Yonder on Calvary's mount out- poured,
Am   G   D7   G
There where the blood of the Lamb was spilt.

Chorus   G   C   G
Grace, grace, God's grace,
D7   G   C   G
Grace that will pardon and cleanse within;
G   C   G
Grace, grace, God's grace,
Am   G   D7   G
Grace that is greater than all   our   sin.

Arr. © Copyright 2010 Universal Music - Brentwood-Benson Publishing (ASCAP)
(Licensing through Music Services). All rights reserved. Used by permission.

Verse 2

```
         G         D7         G  D7  G
         Dark is the stain that we can-not  hide,
         D                   G
         What can avail to wash it away?
         G         D7        G  D7  Em
         Look! There is flowing a crimson  tide;
         Am                     G  D7  G
         Whiter than snow you may be  to-  day.
```

Verse 3

```
         G         D7      G  D7  G
         Marvelous, infinite, matchless  grace,
         D                   G
         Freely bestowed on all who believe;
         G         D7        G  D7  Em
         All who are longing to see  His  face,
         Am                     G  D7  G
         Will you this moment His grace re-  ceive?
```

Great Is Thy Faithfulness

Words by THOMAS O. CHISHOLM
Music by WILLIAM M. RUNYAN

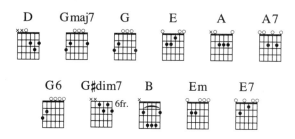

Verse 1
      D   Gmaj7   G   D
Great is Thy faithfulness, O God, my Father;
G   D   E   A
There is no shadow of turning with Thee.
A7   D   Gmaj7 G6
Thou changest not; Thy compassions, they fail   not.
G#dim7   D   A7   D
As Thou hast been Thou forever wilt be.

© Copyright 1923, Renewed 1951 and this Arr. © 2009 Hope Publishing Company (Carol Stream, IL 60188).
All rights reserved. Used by permission.

Chorus

| A | G | D | B | | Em |

Great is Thy faithfulness! Great is Thy faithfulness!

| A7 | D | A | E7 | A |

Morning by morning new mercies I   see;

| A7 | D | | Gmaj7 | G6 |

All I have needed Thy hand hath provid-   ed.

| G♯dim7 | D | | A7 | D |

Great is Thy faithfulness, Lord, unto me!

Verse 2

| D | Gmaj7 | G | | D |

Summer and winter, and springtime and harvest,

| G | D | E | A |

Sun, moon and stars in their courses above,

| A7 | D | | Gmaj7 | G6 |

Join with all nature in manifold wit-   ness

| G♯dim7 | D | | A7 | D |

To Thy great faithfulness, mercy and love.

Verse 3

| D | Gmaj7 | G | | D |

Pardon for sin and a peace that endureth,

| G | D | E | A |

Thine own dear presence to cheer and to guide.

| A7 | D | | Gmaj7 | G6 |

Strength for today and bright hope for tomor-   row

| G♯dim7 | D | | A7 | D |

Blessings all mine with ten thousand beside!

Glorify Thy Name

Words and Music by
DONNA ADKINS

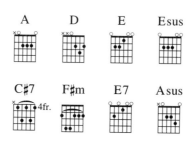

Verse 1
    A   D   E   A
Father, we love You, we worship and adore You,
A   D   Esus E
Glorify Thy name in all the earth.

Chorus
A   D   C#7   F#m
Glorify Thy name, Glorify Thy name,
D   E7   Asus A
Glorify Thy name in all the earth.

Verse 2
A   D   E   A
Jesus, we love You, we worship and adore You,
A   D   Esus E
Glorify Thy name in all the earth.

Verse 3
A   D   E   A
Spirit, we love You, we worship and adore You,
A   D   Esus E
Glorify Thy name in all the earth.

© Copyright 1976, 1981 Maranatha Music / CCCM Music (ASCAP) (Both administered by Music Services).
All rights reserved. Used by permission.

I Love You, Lord

Words and Music by
LAURIE KLEIN

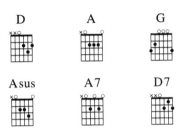

Chorus
        D   A   D
I love You, Lord, and I lift   my voice
     G D   A   D   A   Asus A7
To worship You, O my soul re-   joice!
        D   A   D
Take joy, my King, in what You hear:
D7   G   D   A   A7 D G D
May it be a sweet, sweet sound in Your ear.

© Copyright 1978 House of Mercy Music (ASCAP) (Administered by Music Services o/b/o Maranatha Music).
All rights reserved. Used by permission.

Hallelujah, What a Savior!

Words and Music by
PHILIP P. BLISS

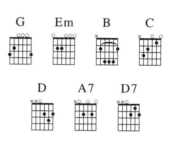

Verse 1
      G   Em   B
"Man of sorrows!" what a name
C   G   D   A7   D
For the Son of God who came
G
Ruined sinners to reclaim!
        G   D7 Em   C   G
Hallelu- jah, what a Savior!

Verse 2
      G   Em   B
Bearing shame and scoffing rude,
C   G   D   A7   D
In my place condemned He stood,
G
Sealed my pardon with His blood;
        G   D7 Em   C   G
Hallelu- jah, what a Savior!

Arr. © Copyright 2010 Universal Music - Brentwood-Benson Publishing (ASCAP)
(Licensing through Music Services). All rights reserved. Used by permission.

Verse 3

```
        G              Em    B
Guilty, vile and helpless we,
       C    G       D   A7  D
Spotless Lamb of God was  He;
G
Full atonement! can it be?
        G   D7  Em   C   G
Hallelu- jah, what a Savior!
```

Verse 4

```
        G          Em   B
Lifted up was He to die,
      C   G        D  A7  D
"It is finished," was His  cry;
G
Now in heav'n exalted high:
        G   D7  Em   C   G
Hallelu- jah, what a Savior!
```

Verse 5

```
        G                Em    B
When He comes, our glorious King,
       C   G         D   A7  D
All His ransomed home to    bring,
G
Then anew this song we'll sing:
        G   D7  Em   C   G
Hallelu- jah, what a Savior!
```

Have Thine Own Way, Lord

Words by ADELAIDE A. POLLARD
Music by GEORGE C. STEBBINS

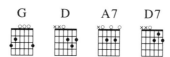

Verse 1

                   G   D   A7
Have Thine own way, Lord! Have Thine own way!
       A7   D
Thou art the Potter, I am the clay!
               G   D D7   G
Mold me and make me After Thy will,
        D   A7   D
While I am waiting, Yielded and still.

Verse 2

                   G   D   A7
Have Thine own way, Lord! Have Thine own way!
      A7   D
Search me and try me, Master, today!
          G   D D7   G
Whiter than snow, Lord, Wash me just now,
     D   A7   D
As in Thy presence Humbly I bow.

Arr. © Copyright 2010 Universal Music - Brentwood-Benson Publishing (ASCAP)
(Licensing through Music Services). All rights reserved. Used by permission.

Verse 3

           G **D**   **A7**
Have Thine own way, Lord! Have Thine own way!
      A7   **D**
Wounded and weary, Help me, I pray!
    G **D** **D7**   **G**
Power, all power   Surely is Thine!
     D   **A7**   **D**
Touch me and heal me, Savior divine.

Verse 4

           G **D**   **A7**
Have Thine own way, Lord! Have Thine own way!
      A7   **D**
Hold o'er my being Absolute sway!
      G **D** **D7**   **G**
Fill with Thy Spirit   Till all shall see
    D   **A7**   **D**
Christ only, always Living in me.

He Hideth My Soul

Words by FANNY CROSBY
Music by WILLIAM J. KIRKPATRICK

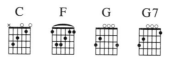

Verse 1
      C   F   C
A wonderful Savior is Jesus my Lord,
      C   G
A wonderful Savior to me;
      C   F
He hideth my soul in the cleft of the rock,
      C   G7   C
Where rivers of pleasure I see.

Chorus
      G7   C
He hideth my soul in the cleft of the rock
      G7   C
That shadows a dry, thirsty land;
      C   F
He hideth my life in the depths of His love
      C   G   C
And covers me there with His hand,
      C   G7   C
And covers me there with His hand.

Arr. © Copyright 2010 Universal Music - Brentwood-Benson Publishing (ASCAP)
(Licensing through Music Services). All rights reserved. Used by permission.

Verse 2
```
             C                  F        C
       A wonderful Savior is Jesus my Lord,
             C              G
       He taketh my burden away;
             C                F
       He holdeth me up, and I shall not be moved,
             C       G7         C
       He giveth me strength as my day.
```

Verse 3
```
              C                    F         C
       With numberless blessings each moment He crowns,
              C                G
       And filled with His fullness divine,
           C             F
       I sing in my rapture, "Oh, glory to God
              C       G7     C
       For such a Redeemer as mine!"
```

Verse 4
```
                 C                    F     C
       When clothed in His brightness, transported I rise
               C                G
       To meet Him in clouds of the sky,
              C              F
       His perfect salvation, His wonderful love
              C        G7       C
       I'll shout with the millions on high!
```

He Keeps Me Singing

Words and Music by
LUTHER B. BRIDGERS

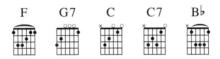

Verse 1
    F   G7
There's within my heart a melody;
C   F   C7
Jesus whispers sweet and low,
    F   G7
"Fear not, I am with thee, peace, be still,"
C7   F
In all of life's ebb and flow.

Chorus
    F   C7
Jesus, Jesus, Jesus,
C7   F
Sweetest name I know,
F   B♭
Fills my every longing,
C7   F
Keeps me singing as I go.

Arr. © Copyright 2010 Universal Music - Brentwood-Benson Publishing (ASCAP)
(Licensing through Music Services). All rights reserved. Used by permission.

Verse 2
    F   G7
All my life was wrecked by sin and strife,
C   F   C7
Discord filled my heart with pain;
F   G7
Jesus swept across the broken strings,
C7   F
Stirred the slumb'ring chords again.

Verse 3
    F   G7
Feasting on the riches of His grace,
C   F   C7
Resting 'neath His shelt'ring wing,
F   G7
Always looking on His smiling face,
C7   F
That is why I shout and sing.

Verse 4
    F   G7
Though sometimes He leads through waters deep,
C   F   C7
Trials fall across the way;
F   G7
Though sometimes the path seems rough and steep,
C7   F
See His footprints all the way.

Verse 5
    F   G7
Soon He's coming back to welcome me
C   F   C7
Far beyond the starry sky;
F   G7
I shall wing my flight to worlds unknown,
C7   F
I shall reign with Him on high.

He Lives!

Words and Music by
A. H. ACKLEY

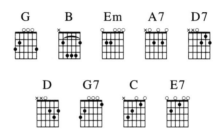

Verse 1 G
I serve a risen Savior, He's in the world today;
G   B   Em   A7   D7
I know that He is living, whatever men may say.
G
I see His hand of mercy, I hear His voice of cheer,
A7   D
And just the time I need Him, He's always near.

Chorus G   G7   C   G
He lives, He lives! Christ Jesus lives today!
D7   G
He walks with me and talks with me
A7   D7
Along life's narrow way.
G   G7   C   B
He lives, He lives, salvation to impart!
E7   A7
You ask me how I know He lives?
G   D7   G
He lives within my heart!

© Copyright 1933 Word Music Group, LLC. All rights reserved. Used by permission.

Verse 2
         G
In all the world around me I see His loving care;
     G   **B**   **Em**   **A7**   **D7**
And though my heart grows weary, I never will despair.
   G
I know that He is leading through all the stormy blast;
 A7   **D**
The day of His appearing will come at last.

Verse 3
         G
Rejoice, rejoice, O Christian, lift up your voice and sing
  G   **B**   **Em**   **A7**   **D7**
Eternal hallelujahs to Jesus Christ, the King!
     G
The Hope of all who seek Him, the Help of all who find,
   A7   **D**
None other is so loving, so good and kind.

He's Got the Whole World in His Hands
Traditional

Verse 1
          C
He's got the whole world in His hands.
          G7
He's got the whole world in His hands.
          C
He's got the whole world in His hands.
          G7   **C**
He's got the whole world in His hands.

Verse 2
          C
He's got the wind and the rain in His hands.
          G7
He's got the wind and the rain in His hands.
          C
He's got the wind and the rain in His hands.
          G7   **C**
He's got the whole world in His hands.

Arr. © Copyright 2010 Universal Music - Brentwood-Benson Publishing (ASCAP)
(Licensing through Music Services). All rights reserved. Used by permission.

Verse 3
                  C
He's got the tiny little baby in His hands.
                  G7
He's got the tiny little baby in His hands.
                  C
He's got the tiny little baby in His hands.
              G7   **C**
He's got the whole world in His hands.

Verse 4
              C
He's got you and me, brother, in His hands.
              G7
He's got you and me, sister, in His hands.
              C
He's got you and me, brother, in His hands.
            G7   **C**
He's got the whole world in His hands.

Heaven Came Down

Words and Music by
JOHN W. PETERSON

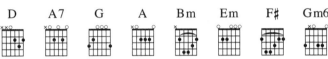

Verse 1   **D**
O what a wonderful, wonderful day—
D   **A7**
Day I will never forget;
A7
After I'd wandered in darkness away,
A7   **D**
Jesus my Savior I met.
D
O what a tender, compassionate friend—
D   **G**
He met the need of my heart;
G   **D**
Shadows dispelling, With joy I am telling,
 A   **A7**   **D**
He made all the darkness depart!

Chorus   **D**   **Bm**   **Em** **A7**   **D G D**
Heaven came down and glory filled my soul,
              D   **Bm**   **Em** **A7**   **D G D Bm**
When at the cross the Savior made me whole;
              Em
My sins were washed away—
              D   **F♯**   **Bm** **Gm6**
And my night was turned to day—
              D   **Bm**   **Em** **A7**   **D G D**
Heaven came down and glory filled my soul!

© Copyright 1961 by John W. Peterson Music Company. All rights reserved. Used by permission.

Verse 2

```
         D
Born of the Spirit with life from above
         D              A7
Into God's family divine,
A7
Justified fully through Calvary's love,
A7              D
Oh, what a standing is mine!
D
And the transaction so quickly was made
         D        G
When as a sinner I came,
G              D
Took of the offer of grace He did proffer–
    A       A7        D
He saved me, O praise His dear name!
```

Verse 3

```
         D
Now I've a hope that will surely endure
         D         A7
After the passing of time;
A7
I have a future in heaven for sure,
A7                   D
There in those mansions sublime.
D
And it's because of that wonderful day
         D          G
When at the cross I believed;
G              D
Riches eternal and blessings supernal
         A       A7    D
From His precious hand I received.
```

Higher Ground

Words by JOHNSON OATMAN, JR.
Music by CHARLES H. GABRIEL

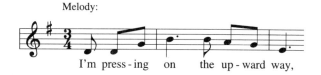

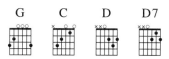

Verse 1
           G   **C**
I'm pressing on the upward way,
           G   **D**
New heights I'm gaining every day;
           G   **C**
Still praying as I onward bound,
           G   **D7** **G**
"Lord, plant my feet on higher   ground."

Chorus
           G   **D7**
Lord, lift me up and let me stand,
       D7   **G**
By faith, on heaven's tableland;
       G   **C**
A higher plane than I have found;
         G   **D7** **G**
Lord, plant my feet on higher   ground.

Arr. © Copyright 2010 Universal Music - Brentwood-Benson Publishing (ASCAP)
(Licensing through Music Services). All rights reserved. Used by permission.

Verse 2

     G   C
  My heart has no desire to stay
      G   D
  Where doubts arise and fears dismay;
       G   C
  Though some may dwell where these abound,
      G D7 G
  My prayer, my aim is higher ground.

Verse 3

     G   C
  I want to live above the world,
      G   D
  Though Satan's darts at me are hurled;
      G   C
  For faith has caught the joyful sound,
      G   D7 G
  The song of saints on higher ground.

Verse 4

     G   C
  I want to scale the utmost height
      G   D
  And catch a gleam of glory bright;
      G   C
  But still I'll pray till heaven I've found,
      G D7 G
  "Lord, lead me on to higher ground."

His Eye Is on the Sparrow

Words by CIVILLA D. MARTIN
Music by CHARLES H. GABRIEL

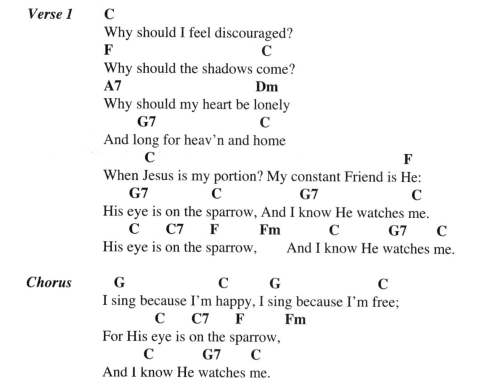

Verse 1
C
Why should I feel discouraged?
F   C
Why should the shadows come?
A7   Dm
Why should my heart be lonely
       G7   C
And long for heav'n and home
       C   F
When Jesus is my portion? My constant Friend is He:
   G7   C   G7   C
His eye is on the sparrow, And I know He watches me.
     C   C7   F   Fm   C   G7   C
His eye is on the sparrow,   And I know He watches me.

Chorus
G   C   G   C
I sing because I'm happy, I sing because I'm free;
     C   C7   F   Fm
For His eye is on the sparrow,
       C   G7   C
And I know He watches me.

Arr. © Copyright 2010 Universal Music - Brentwood-Benson Publishing (ASCAP)
(Licensing through Music Services). All rights reserved. Used by permission.

Verse 2

```
        C                              F                  C
       "Let not your heart be troubled," His tender words I hear;
        A7          Dm           G7                   C
       And resting on His goodness, I lose my doubt and fear.
                    C                                   F
       Though by the path He leadeth But one step I may see:
            G7          C           G7              C
       His eye is on the sparrow, And I know He watches me.
            C    C7    F      Fm         C       G7    C
       His eye is on the sparrow,    And I know He watches me.
```

Verse 3

```
        C                     F             C
       Whenever I am tempted, Whenever clouds arise,
        A7                   Dm
       When songs give place to sighing,
        G7               C
       When hope within me dies,
           C                                     F
       I draw the closer to Him; From care He sets me free:
            G7          C           G7              C
       His eye is on the sparrow, And I know He watches me.
            C    C7    F      Fm         C       G7    C
       His eye is on the sparrow,    And I know He watches me.
```

Holy, Holy, Holy!

Words by REGINALD HEBER
Music by JOHN B. DYKES

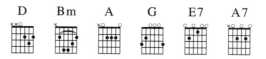

Verse 1
D   Bm A D G   D
Holy, holy, ho- ly! Lord God Almighty!
A   Bm A   E7 A A7
Early in the morn-ing our song shall rise to Thee;
D   Bm A D G   D
Holy, holy, ho- ly! merciful and mighty!
Bm D   G D G   A7 D
God in three Per- sons, blessed Trini- ty!

Verse 2
D   Bm A D G   D
Holy, holy, ho- ly! all the saints adore Thee,
A   Bm A   E7 A A7
Casting down their golden crowns around the glassy sea;
D   Bm A D G   D
Cherubim and seraphim falling down before Thee,
Bm D   G D G A7   D
Who wert, and art, and evermore shalt be.

Arr. © Copyright 2010 Universal Music - Brentwood-Benson Publishing (ASCAP)
(Licensing through Music Services). All rights reserved. Used by permission.

Verse 3
    D   Bm A D G   D
Holy, holy, ho- ly! though the darkness hide Thee,
A   Bm A   E7   A A7
Though the eye of sinful man Thy glory may not see;
D   Bm A D G   D
Only Thou art ho- ly; there is none beside Thee,
Bm D   G   D G   A7 D
Per- fect in power, in love and puri- ty.

Verse 4
    D   Bm A D G   D
Holy, holy, ho- ly! Lord God Almighty!
A   Bm   A
All Thy works shall praise Thy name,
  A   E7   A A7
In earth, and sky, and sea;
D   Bm A D G   D
Holy, holy, ho- ly! merciful and mighty!
Bm D   G D   G   A7 D
God in three Per- sons, blessed Trini- ty!

How Great Thou Art

Words and Music by
STUART K. HINE

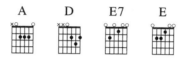

Verse 1
        A   **D**
O Lord, my God, when I in awesome wonder
        A   **E7**   **A**
Consider all the worlds Thy hands have made,
        A   **D**
I see the stars, I hear the rolling thunder,
             A   **E7**   **A**
Thy pow'r throughout the universe displayed.

Chorus
           A   **D**   **A**
Then sings my soul, my Savior God, to Thee,
    E7   **A**
How great Thou art! How great Thou art!
           A   **D**   **A**
Then sings my soul, my Savior God, to Thee;
  E **A**   **D**   **E7**   **A**
How great Thou art! How great Thou art!

© Copyright 1953 S. K. Hine. Renewed 1981. Administrator: Manna Music, Inc. (ASCAP)
(35255 Brooten Road, Pacific City, OR 97135). All rights reserved. Used by permission.

Verse 2

              A   D
When thro' the woods and forest glades I wander
          A   E7   A
And hear the birds sing sweetly in the trees,
        A   D
When I look down from lofty mountain grandeur,
        A   E7   A
And hear the brook and feel the gentle breeze;

Verse 3

           A   D
And when I think that God, His Son not sparing,
       A   E7   A
Sent Him to die, I scarce can take it in;
       A   D
That on the cross, my burden gladly bearing,
      A   E7   A
He bled and died to take away my sin.

Verse 4

          A   D
When Christ shall come with shout of acclamation
        A   E7   A
And take me home, what joy shall fill my heart!
     A   D
Then I shall bow in humble adoration
         A   E7   A
And there proclaim: my God, how great Thou art!

I Am Thine, O Lord

Words by FANNY CROSBY
Music by WILLIAM H. DOANE

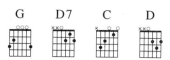

Verse 1
       G   D7   G
I am Thine, O Lord, I have heard Thy voice,
     C   G
And it told Thy love to me.
       G   D7   G
But I long to rise in the arms of faith,
     C   D   G
And be closer drawn to Thee.

Chorus
          G   C   G
Draw me nearer, nearer, blessed Lord,
   C   D
To the cross where Thou hast died.
      G   C
Draw me nearer, nearer, nearer, blessed Lord,
    G   D7   G
To Thy precious, bleeding side.

Verse 2
        G   D7   G
Consecrate me now to Thy service, Lord,
     C   G
By the power of grace divine.
        G   D7   G
Let my soul look up with a steadfast hope,
    C   D   G
And my will be lost in Thine.

Verse 3
        G   D7   G
O the pure delight of a single hour
     C   G
That before Thy throne I spend;
        G   D7   G
When I kneel in prayer, and with Thee, my God,
    C   D   G
I commune as friend with friend!

Verse 4
        G   D7   G
There are depths of love that I cannot know
    C   G
Till I cross the narrow sea;
        G   D7   G
There are heights of joy that I may not reach
    C   D   G
Till I rest in peace with Thee.

I Have Decided to Follow Jesus
Traditional

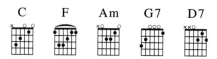

Verse 1
        C
I have decided to follow Jesus;
      F   C
I have decided to follow Jesus;
      C   Am
I have decided to follow Jesus;
  G7   C   D7   G7   C
No turning back,   no turning back.

Verse 2
            C
Though none go with me, I still will follow;
            F   C
Though none go with me, I still will follow;
            C   Am
Though none go with me, I still will follow;
  G7   C   D7   G7   C
No turning back,   no turning back.

Arr. © Copyright 2010 Universal Music - Brentwood-Benson Publishing (ASCAP)
(Licensing through Music Services). All rights reserved. Used by permission.

Verse 3

      C
My cross I'll carry, till I see Jesus;
     F   **C**
My cross I'll carry, till I see Jesus;
      C   **Am**
My cross I'll carry, till I see Jesus;
G7 **C** **D7** **G7** **C**
No turning back, no turning back.

Verse 4

      C
The world behind me, the cross before me;
     F   **C**
The world behind me, the cross before me;
     C   **Am**
The world behind me, the cross before me;
G7 **C** **D7** **G7** **C**
No turning back, no turning back.

I Love to Tell the Story

Words by KATHERINE HANKEY
Music by WILLIAM G. FISCHER

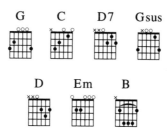

Verse 1
        G   C   G
I love to tell the story Of unseen things above,
    D7   Gsus G   D
Of Jesus and His glo-   ry, Of Jesus and His love.
    D7   Gsus G Em   B
I love to tell the sto-   ry Because I know 'tis true;
    C   G   D7   G
It satisfies my longings As nothing else can do.

Chorus   D7   Gsus G
I love to tell the sto-   ry,
        C   Gsus G
'Twill be my theme in glo- ry
    G   C   G   D7   G
To tell the old, old story Of Jesus and His love.

Arr. © Copyright 2010 Universal Music - Brentwood-Benson Publishing (ASCAP)
(Licensing through Music Services). All rights reserved. Used by permission.

Verse 2

```
        G                        C            G
I love to tell the story; 'Tis pleasant to repeat
        D7             Gsus  G                D
What seems each time I tell   it, More wonderfully sweet.
        D7         Gsus  G     Em             B
I love to tell the sto-   ry, For some have never heard
        C          G          D7          G
The message of salvation From God's own holy Word.
```

Verse 3

```
        G                     C              G
I love to tell the story; For those who know it best
        D7         Gsus  G                      D
Seem hungering and thirst- ing To hear it, like the rest.
        D7              Gsus  G    Em             B
And when, in scenes of glo-   ry, I sing the new, new song,
        C             G       D7             G
'Twill be the old, old story That I have loved so long.
```

I Stand Amazed in the Presence

Words and Music by
CHARLES H. GABRIEL

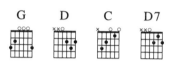

Verse 1   G
I stand amazed in the presence
     D   G
Of Jesus the Nazarene,
    C   G
And wonder how He could love me,
  G   D7   G
A sinner, condemned, unclean.

Chorus   G
How marvelous! How wonderful!
D   D7
And my song shall ever be;
G
How marvelous! How wonderful!
C   G   D7 G
Is my Savior's love for me!

Arr. © Copyright 2010 Universal Music - Brentwood-Benson Publishing (ASCAP)
(Licensing through Music Services). All rights reserved. Used by permission.

Verse 2

    G
For me it was in the garden
    D   G
He prayed, "Not My will, but Thine."
    C   G
He had no tears for His own griefs,
    G   D7   G
But sweat drops of blood for mine.

Verse 3

    G
He took my sins and my sorrows,
    D   G
He made them His very own.
    C   G
He bore the burden to Calv'ry,
    G   D7   G
And suffered and died alone.

Verse 4

       G
When with the ransomed in glory
    D   G
His face I at last shall see,
    C   G
'Twill be my joy through the ages
    G   D7   G
To sing of His love for me.

I Surrender All

Words by JUDSON VAN DEVENTER
Music by WINFIELD S. WEEDEN

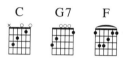

Verse 1
    C   **G7**
All to Jesus I surrender,
C   **G7** **C**
All to Him I freely give;
C   **G7**
I will ever love and trust Him,
C   **G7** **C**
In His presence daily live.

Chorus
   C   **G7**
I surrender all,
G7   **C**
I surrender all;
C   **F**
All to Thee, my blessed Savior,
C **G7** **C**
I surrender all.

Arr. © Copyright 2010 Universal Music - Brentwood-Benson Publishing (ASCAP)
(Licensing through Music Services). All rights reserved. Used by permission.

Verse 2   C   G7
All to Jesus I surrender,
C   G7   C
Humbly at His feet I bow,
C   G7
Worldly pleasures all forsaken,
C   G7   C
Take me, Jesus, take me now.

Verse 3   C   G7
All to Jesus I surrender,
C   G7   C
Make me, Savior, wholly Thine;
C   G7
May Thy Holy Spirit fill me,
C   G7   C
May I know Thy pow'r divine.

Verse 4   C   G7
All to Jesus I surrender,
C   G7   C
Lord, I give myself to Thee;
C   G7
Fill me with Thy love and power,
C   G7   C
Let Thy blessing fall on me.

I Need Thee Every Hour

Words by ANNIE S. HAWKS
Music by ROBERT LOWRY

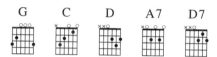

Verse 1
      G   C   G
I need Thee every hour, Most gracious Lord;
  D   G   A7   D
No tender voice like Thine Can peace afford.

Chorus
     G   D   G
I need Thee, O I need Thee; Every hour I need Thee!
  C   G   D7   G
O bless me now, my Savior, I come to Thee.

Verse 2
      G   C   G
I need Thee every hour, Stay Thou nearby;
  D   G   A7   D
Temptations lose their pow'r When Thou art nigh.

Verse 3
      G   C   G
I need Thee every hour, In joy or pain;
  D   G   A7   D
Come quickly and abide, Or life is vain.

Verse 4
      G   C   G
I need Thee every hour, Teach me Thy will;
  D   G   A7   D
Thy promises so rich in me fulfill.

Arr. © Copyright 2010 Universal Music - Brentwood-Benson Publishing (ASCAP)
(Licensing through Music Services). All rights reserved. Used by permission.

I've Got Peace like a River
Traditional

Verse 1

      G   G7   C   G
I've got peace like a river, I've got peace like a river,
      G   D7
I've got peace like a river in my soul;
      G   G7   C   G
I've got peace like a river, I've got peace like a river,
      G   A7   D7   G C G
I've got peace like a river in my soul.

Verse 2

      G   G7   C   G
I've got love like an ocean, I've got love like an ocean,
      G   D7
I've got love like an ocean in my soul;
      G   G7   C   G
I've got love like an ocean, I've got love like an ocean,
      G   A7   D7   G C G
I've got love like an ocean in my soul.

Verse 3

      G   G7   C   G
I've got joy like a fountain, I've got joy like a fountain,
      G   D7
I've got joy like a fountain in my soul;
      G   G7   C   G
I've got joy like a fountain, I've got joy like a fountain,
      G   A7   D7   G C G
I've got joy like a fountain in my soul.

Arr. © Copyright 2010 Universal Music - Brentwood-Benson Publishing (ASCAP)
(Licensing through Music Services). All rights reserved. Used by permission.

Immortal, Invisible, God Only Wise

Words by WALTER C. SMITH
Music: Welsh Melody

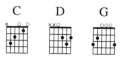

Verse 1
       C   D   G   D G
Immortal, invisible, God only wise,
       C   D   G   D G
In light inaccessible hid from our eyes,
       G   D
Most blessed, most glorious, the Ancient of Days,
       C   D   G   D G
Almighty, victorious, Thy great name we praise.

Verse 2
       C   D   G   D G
Unresting, unhasting, and silent as light,
       C   D   G   D G
Not wanting, nor wasting, Thou rulest in might;
       G   D
Thy justice, like mountains, high soaring above
       C   D   G   D G
Thy clouds, which are fountains of goodness and love.

Arr. © Copyright 2010 Universal Music - Brentwood-Benson Publishing (ASCAP)
(Licensing through Music Services). All rights reserved. Used by permission.

Verse 3
```
           C         D        G       D  G
```
To all, life Thou givest, to both great and small;
```
           C         D       G       D  G
```
In all life Thou livest, the true life of   all;
```
           G                           D
```
We blossom and flourish as leaves on the tree,
```
           C         D         G        D  G
```
And wither and perish– but naught changeth Thee.

Verse 4
```
           C      D       G    D G
```
Great Father of glory, pure Father of   light,
```
           C      D         G    D  G
```
Thine angels adore Thee, all veiling their sight;
```
           G                           D
```
All praise we would render; O help us to see
```
           C        D        G     D  G
```
'Tis only the splendor of light hideth Thee!

In the Garden

Words and Music by
C. AUSTIN MILES

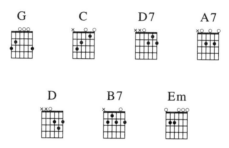

Verse 1

      G
I come to the garden alone,
    C   **G**
While the dew is still on the roses;
    D7   **G**
And the voice I hear, falling on my ear,
  A7   **D** **D7**
The Son of God disclos- es.

Arr. © Copyright 2010 Universal Music - Brentwood-Benson Publishing (ASCAP)
(Licensing through Music Services). All rights reserved. Used by permission.

Chorus

        G   **D7**
And He walks with me, and He talks with me,
    D7   **G**
And He tells me I am His own,
       G   **B7**   **Em** **C**
And the joy we share as we tarry there,
      G   **D7** **G**
None other has ever known.

Verse 2

    G
He speaks, and the sound of His voice
     C   **G**
Is so sweet, the birds hush their singing;
    D7   **G**
And the melody that He gave to me
   A7   **D** **D7**
Within my heart is ringing.

Verse 3

    G
I'd stay in the garden with Him
       C   **G**
Though the night around me be falling;
    D7   **G**
But He bids me go, through the voice of woe,
   A7   **D** **D7**
His voice to me is call-ing.

In the Sweet By and By

Words by SANFORD F. BENNETT
Music by JOSEPH P. WEBSTER

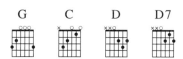

Verse 1
        G   **C**   **G**
There's a land that is fairer than day,
    G   **D**
And by faith we can see it afar;
   G   **C**   **G**
For the Father waits over the way
   G   **D**   **G**
To prepare us a dwelling place there.

Chorus
     G   **D**
In the sweet by and by,
  D7   **G**
We shall meet on that beautiful shore;
   G   **C**
In the sweet by and by,
   G   **D7**   **G**
We shall meet on that beautiful shore.

Arr. © Copyright 2010 Universal Music - Brentwood-Benson Publishing (ASCAP)
(Licensing through Music Services). All rights reserved. Used by permission.

Verse 2
```
           G         C        G
We shall sing on that beautiful shore
           G                 D
The melodious songs of the blest,
             G        C        G
And our spirits shall sorrow no more,
           G         D        G
Not a sigh for the blessing of rest.
```

Verse 3
```
              G        C     G
To our bountiful Father above,
              G                D
We will offer the tribute of praise
             G         C      G
For the glorious gift of His love,
             G          D        G
And the blessings that hallow our days.
```

It Is Well with My Soul

Words by HORATIO SPAFFORD
Music by PHILIP P. BLISS

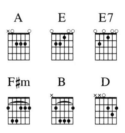

Verse 1
            A   **E**   **E7**   **A**
When peace, like a river, attendeth my way,
       F♯m   **B**   **E**
When sorrows like sea billows roll;
         A   **D**   **B**   **E**
Whatever my lot, Thou hast taught me to say,
        A   **E**   **A**
"It is well, it is well with my soul."

Chorus
        A   **E**   **E7**   **A**
It is well (It is well) with my soul, (with my soul,)
     D   **A E**   **A**
It is well, it is well with my soul.

Verse 2

     A   E   E7   A
  Though Satan should buffet, though trials should come,
   F♯m   B   E
  Let this blest assurance control,
   A   D   B   E
  That Christ has regarded my helpless estate,
   A   E   A
  And hath shed His own blood for my soul.

Verse 3

   A   E E7   A
  My sin– oh, the bliss of this glorious thought:
   F♯m   B   E
  My sin– not in part, but the whole
   A   D   B   E
  Is nailed to the cross and I bear it no more,
   A   E   A
  Praise the Lord, praise the Lord, O my soul!

Verse 4

   A   E   E7   A
  And, Lord, haste the day when the faith shall be sight,
   F♯m   B   E
  The clouds be rolled back as a scroll,
   A   D   B   E
  The trump shall resound and the Lord shall descend,
   A   E   A
  "Even so," it is well with my soul.

Jesus, Keep Me Near the Cross

Words by FANNY CROSBY
Music by WILLIAM H. DOANE

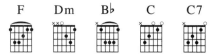

Verse 1
    F   **Dm**   **B♭**
Jesus, keep me near the cross,
F   **C**
There a precious fountain,
F   **Dm**   **B♭**
Free to all, a healing stream,
F   **C7** **F**
Flows from Calvary's mountain.

Chorus
    F   **B♭**
In the cross, in the cross
F   **C**
Be my glory ever,
F   **B♭**
Till my ransomed soul shall find
F   **C7** **F**
Rest beyond the riv- er.

Arr. © Copyright 2010 Universal Music - Brentwood-Benson Publishing (ASCAP)
(Licensing through Music Services). All rights reserved. Used by permission.

Verse 2

F	Dm	B♭

Near the cross, a trembling soul,

F		C	

Love and mercy found me;

F	Dm	B♭

There the Bright and Morning Star

F	C7	F

Shed His beams around me.

Verse 3

F	Dm	B♭

Near the cross! O Lamb of God,

F		C	

Bring its scenes before me;

F	Dm	B♭

Help me walk from day to day

F	C7	F

With its shadow o'er me.

Verse 4

F	Dm	B♭

Near the cross! I'll watch and wait,

F		C	

Hoping, trusting ever,

F	Dm	B♭

Till I reach the golden strand,

F	C7	F

Just beyond the riv- er.

Jesus Loves Me

Words by ANNA B. WARNER
Music by WILLIAM B. BRADBURY

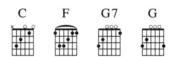

Verse 1
    C
Jesus loves me! this I know,
F   **C**
For the Bible tells me so;
C
Little ones to Him belong;
F   **C**   **G7**   **C**
They are weak, but He is strong.

Chorus
    C   **F**
Yes, Jesus loves me,
C   **G**
Yes, Jesus loves me,
C   **F**
Yes, Jesus loves me,
   C **G7**   **C**
The Bible tells me so.

Arr. © Copyright 2010 Universal Music - Brentwood-Benson Publishing (ASCAP)
(Licensing through Music Services). All rights reserved. Used by permission.

Verse 2

```
           C
           Jesus loves me! He who died
           F                    C
           Heaven's gates to open wide!
           C
           He will wash away my sin,
           F      C    G7       C
           Let His little child come in.
```

Verse 3

```
           C
           Jesus loves me! loves me still,
           F                        C
           Though I'm very weak and ill;
           C
           From His shining throne on high,
           F      C     G7      C
           Comes to watch me where I lie.
```

Verse 4

```
           C
           Jesus loves me! He will stay
           F                   C
           Close beside me all the way;
           C
           If I love Him, when I die
           F      C     G7      C
           He will take me home on high.
```

Jesus Paid It All

Words by ELVINA M. HALL
Music by JOHN T. GRAPE

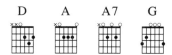

Verse 1   **D**
I hear the Savior say,
     A   **D**
"Thy strength indeed is small,
   D
Child of weakness, watch and pray,
     D   **A7** **D**
Find in Me thine all in all."

Chorus   **D**
Jesus paid it all,
  D   **A**
All to Him I owe;
  D   **G**
Sin had left a crimson stain,
    D   **A7**   **D**
He washed it white as snow.

Arr. © Copyright 2010 Universal Music - Brentwood-Benson Publishing (ASCAP)
(Licensing through Music Services). All rights reserved. Used by permission.

Verse 2

      D
Lord, now indeed I find
  A   **D**
Thy power, and Thine alone
D
Can change the leper's spots
  D   **A7**   **D**
And melt the heart of stone.

Verse 3

    D
For nothing good have I
  A   **D**
Whereby Thy grace to claim;
D
I'll wash my garments white
    D   **A7**   **D**
In the blood of Calv'ry's Lamb.

Verse 4

   D
And when, before the throne,
  A   **D**
I stand in Him complete,
   D
"Jesus died my soul to save,"
  D   **A7** **D**
My lips shall still repeat.

Jesus Saves!

Words by PRISCILLA J. OWENS
Music by WILLIAM J. KIRKPATRICK

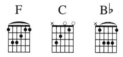

Verse 1

        F   **C**
We have heard the joyful sound: Jesus saves! Jesus saves!
     F   **C**   **F**
Spread the tidings all around: Jesus saves! Jesus saves!
  B♭
Bear the news to every land,
     F   **C**
Climb the steeps and cross the waves;
    F   **B♭**   **C**   **F**
Onward! 'tis our Lord's command; Jesus saves! Jesus saves!

Verse 2

    F   **C**
Waft it on the rolling tide: Jesus saves! Jesus saves!
F   **C**   **F**
Tell to sinners far and wide: Jesus saves! Jesus saves!
 B♭
Sing, ye islands of the sea;
 F   **C**
Echo back, ye ocean caves;
   F   **B♭**   **C**   **F**
Earth shall keep her jubilee: Jesus saves! Jesus saves!

Arr. © Copyright 2010 Universal Music - Brentwood-Benson Publishing (ASCAP)
(Licensing through Music Services). All rights reserved. Used by permission.

Verse 3

         F   **C**
Sing above the battle strife: Jesus saves! Jesus saves!
        F   **C**   **F**
By His death and endless life Jesus saves! Jesus saves!
   B♭
Sing it softly through the gloom,
        F   **C**
When the heart for mercy craves;
       F   **B♭**   **C**   **F**
Sing in triumph o'er the tomb: Jesus saves! Jesus saves!

Verse 4

       F   **C**
Give the winds a mighty voice: Jesus saves! Jesus saves!
     F   **C**   **F**
Let the nations now rejoice: Jesus saves! Jesus saves!
  B♭
Shout salvation full and free;
     F   **C**
Highest hills and deepest caves;
      F   **B♭**   **C**   **F**
This our song of victory: Jesus saves! Jesus saves!

Jesus! What a Friend for Sinners

Words by J. WILBUR CHAPMAN
Music by ROWLAND H. PRICHARD

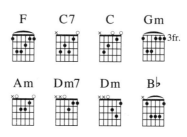

Verse 1
F   C7
Jesus! what a friend for sinners!
F   C   F   Gm   C   F
Je- sus! Lover of   my soul;
F   C7
Friends may fail me, foes assail me,
F   C   F   Gm   C   F
He, my Savior, makes me whole.

Chorus
Am   Dm7   Gm   C7
Halle-lujah! what a Savior!
F   Dm   Gm   C
Hallelujah! what a friend!
F   C7   F   C7
Saving, helping, keeping, loving,
F   B♭   F   C   F
He is with me to   the end.

Arr. © Copyright 2010 Universal Music - Brentwood-Benson Publishing (ASCAP)
(Licensing through Music Services). All rights reserved. Used by permission.

Verse 2
    F   **C7**
    Jesus! what a strength in weakness!
    F **C** **F**   **Gm** **C** **F**
    Let me hide myself in Him;
    F   **C7**
    Tempted, tried, and sometimes failing,
    F **C** **F**   **Gm** **C** **F**
    He, my strength, my vic- t'ry wins.

Verse 3
    F   **C7**
    Jesus! what a help in sorrow!
    F **C** **F**   **Gm** **C** **F**
    While the billows o'er me roll,
    F   **C7**
    Even when my heart is breaking,
    F **C** **F**   **Gm** **C** **F**
    He, my comfort, helps my soul.

Verse 4
    F   **C7**
    Jesus! what a guide and keeper!
    F **C** **F**   **Gm** **C** **F**
    While the tempest still is high,
    F   **C7**
    Storms about me, night o'ertakes me,
    F **C** **F**   **Gm** **C** **F**
    He, my pilot, hears my cry.

Verse 5
    F   **C7**
    Jesus! I do now receive Him,
    F **C** **F**   **Gm** **C** **F**
    More than all in Him I find;
    F   **C7**
    He hath granted me forgiveness,
    F **C** **F**   **Gm** **C** **F**
    I am His, and He is mine.

Joyful, Joyful, We Adore Thee

Words by HENRY J. VAN DYKE
Music by LUDWIG VAN BEETHOVEN

Verse 1

F   C
Joyful, joyful, we adore Thee, God of glory, Lord of love;
F   Bb
Hearts unfold like flowers before Thee,
F   C7   F
Opening to the sun above.
C   F   C   F
Melt the clouds of sin and sadness;
C   A7   Dm   G   C
Drive the dark of doubt a- way;
F   Bb   F   C7   F
Giver of immortal gladness, Fill us with the light of day!

Verse 2

F
All Thy works with joy surround Thee,
F   C
Earth and heaven reflect Thy rays,
F   Bb
Stars and angels sing around Thee,
F   C7   F
Center of unbroken praise.
C   F   C   F
Field and forest, vale and mountain,
C   A7   Dm   G   C
Flowery meadow, flash- ing sea,
F   Bb   F   C7   F
Singing bird and flowing fountain Call us to rejoice in Thee!

Arr. © Copyright 2010 Universal Music - Brentwood-Benson Publishing (ASCAP)
(Licensing through Music Services). All rights reserved. Used by permission.

Verse 3
    F
Thou art giving and forgiving,
    F   C
Ever blessing, ever blest,
    F   Bb
Well-spring of the joy of living,
    F   C7   F
Ocean-depth of happy rest!
C   F   C   F
Thou our Father, Christ our Brother–
C   A7   Dm   G   C
All who live in love are Thine;
    F   Bb   F   C7   F
Teach us how to love each other, Lift us to the joy divine!

Verse 4
    F
Mortals, join the mighty chorus
    F   C
Which the morning stars began;
    F   Bb
Love divine is reigning o'er us,
    F   C7   F
Leading us with mercy's hand.
C   F   C   F
Ever singing, march we onward,
C   A7   Dm   G   C
Victors in the midst of strife.
    F   Bb   F   C7   F
Joyful music leads us sunward In the triumph song of life!

Just a Closer Walk with Thee

Traditional

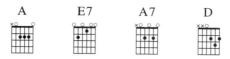

Verse 1
    A   E7
I am weak but Thou art strong;
E7   A
Jesus, keep me from all wrong;
A   A7   D
I'll be satisfied as long
        A   E7   A
As I walk, let me walk close to Thee.

Chorus
    A   E7
Just a closer walk with Thee,
E7   A
Grant it, Jesus, is my plea,
A   A7   D
Daily walking close to Thee,
    A   E7   A
Let it be, dear Lord, let it be.

Arr. © Copyright 2010 Universal Music - Brentwood-Benson Publishing (ASCAP)
(Licensing through Music Services). All rights reserved. Used by permission.

Verse 2

A			E7

Through this world of toil and snares,

E7 **A**

If I falter, Lord, who cares?

A **A7** **D**

Who with me my burden shares?

A **E7** **A**

None but Thee, dear Lord, none but Thee.

Verse 3

A **E7**

When my feeble life is o'er,

E7 **A**

Time for me will be no more;

A **A7** **D**

Guide me gently, safely o'er

A **E7** **A**

To Thy kingdom shore, to Thy shore.

Just As I Am

Words by CHARLOTTE ELLIOTT
Music by WILLLIAM B. BRADBURY

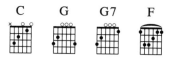

Verse 1
       C   G   C
Just as I am, without one plea,
  G   G7   F   C
But that Thy blood was shed for me,
    C   F
And that Thou bidd'st me come to Thee,
     C   G   C
O Lamb of God, I come! I come!

Verse 2
       C   G   C
Just as I am, and waiting not
  G   G7   F   C
To rid my soul of one dark blot,
    C   F
To Thee whose blood can cleanse each spot,
     C   G   C
O Lamb of God, I come! I come!

Arr. © Copyright 2010 Universal Music - Brentwood-Benson Publishing (ASCAP)
(Licensing through Music Services). All rights reserved. Used by permission.

Verse 3

```
         C              G     C
Just as I am, though tossed about
       G    G7    F      C
With many a conflict, many a doubt,
         C           F
Fightings within and fears without,
       C          G     C
O Lamb of God, I come! I come!
```

Verse 4

```
         C              G     C
Just as I am, poor, wretched, blind;
       G    G7    F      C
Sight, riches, healing of the mind,
         C        F
Yea, all I need in Thee to find,
       C          G     C
O Lamb of God, I come! I come!
```

Verse 5

```
         C              G     C
Just as I am, Thou wilt receive,
       G      G7    F        C
Wilt welcome, pardon, cleanse, relieve.
         C           F
Because Thy promise I believe,
       C          G     C
O Lamb of God, I come! I come!
```

Verse 6

```
         C              G     C
Just as I am, Thy love unknown
       G    G7   F      C
Hath broken every barrier down;
         C           F
Now to be Thine, yea, Thine alone,
       C          G     C
O Lamb of God, I come! I come!
```

Leaning on the Everlasting Arms

Words by ELISHA A. HOFFMAN
Music by ANTHONY J. SHOWALTER

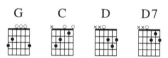

Verse 1
    G   C
What a fellowship, what a joy divine,
G   D
Leaning on the everlasting arms;
G   C
What a blessedness, what a peace is mine,
G   D7 G
Leaning on the everlasting arms.

Chorus
    G   C
Leaning, leaning,
G   D
Safe and secure from all alarms;
G   C
Leaning, leaning,
G   D7 G
Leaning on the everlasting arms.

Arr. © Copyright 2010 Universal Music - Brentwood-Benson Publishing (ASCAP)
(Licensing through Music Services). All rights reserved. Used by permission.

Verse 2
```
        G                       C
        Oh, how sweet to walk in this pilgrim way,
        G                       D
        Leaning on the everlasting arms;
        G                       C
        Oh, how bright the path grows from day to day,
        G                  D7   G
        Leaning on the everlasting   arms.
```

Verse 3
```
        G                       C
        What have I to dread, what have I to fear,
        G                       D
        Leaning on the everlasting arms?
        G                       C
        I have blessed peace with my Lord so near,
        G                  D7   G
        Leaning on the everlasting   arms.
```

Let Us Break Bread Together

Traditional

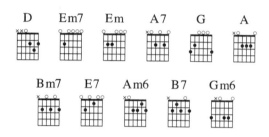

Verse 1
     D Em7 D Em A7 D G D
Let us break bread together on our knees,
     D A Bm7 E7 A D A7
Let us break bread together on our knees;

Chorus
     D Am6 B7   Em Gm6 A7
When I fall on my knees, With my face to the rising sun,
     D Bm7 Em7 A7 D G D
O Lord, have   mercy   on   me.

Verse 2
     D   Em7 D Em A7 D G D
Let us drink the cup together on our knees,
     D A Bm7 E7 A D A7
Let us drink the cup together on our knees;

Verse 3
     D   Em7 D Em A7 D G D
Let us praise God together on our knees,
     D A Bm7 E7 A D A7
Let us praise God together on our knees;

Arr. © Copyright 2010 Universal Music - Brentwood-Benson Publishing (ASCAP)
(Licensing through Music Services). All rights reserved. Used by permission.

Near to the Heart of God

Words and Music by
CLELAND B. McAFEE

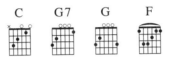

Verse 1
```
         C           G7        G              C
There is a place of quiet rest, Near to the heart of God;
         C              G7         G             C
A place where sin cannot molest, Near to the heart of God.
```

Chorus
```
         F              C  G7              C
O Jesus, blest Redeemer, Sent from the heart of God,
         F            C         G7            C
Hold us who wait before Thee Near to the heart of God.
```

Verse 2
```
         C           G7          G              C
There is a place of comfort sweet, Near to the heart of God;
         C            G7           G             C
A place where we our Savior meet, Near to the heart of God.
```

Verse 3
```
         C           G7         G              C
There is a place of full release, Near to the heart of God;
         C              G7          G             C
A place where all is joy and peace, Near to the heart of God.
```

Arr. © Copyright 2010 Universal Music - Brentwood-Benson Publishing (ASCAP)
(Licensing through Music Services). All rights reserved. Used by permission.

My Faith Has Found a Resting Place

Words by LIDIE H. EDMUNDS
Music: Norwegian Melody

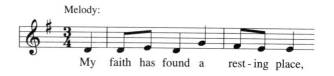

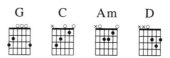

Verse 1
        G   C
My faith has found a resting place,
   Am **G** **D** **G**
Not in device nor creed;
        G   C
I trust the Ever-living One,
     Am   **G** **D**   **G**
His wounds for me shall plead.

Chorus
        G   D
I need no other argument,
      G   C   G D
I need no other plea;
        G   C
It is enough that Jesus died,
   Am   **G** **D**   **G**
And that He died for me.

Verse 2
        G   **C**
Enough for me that Jesus saves,
    Am   **G** **D** **G**
This ends my fear and doubt;
      G   **C**
A sinful soul I come to Him,
  Am **G**   **D** **G**
He'll never cast me out.

Verse 3
      G   **C**
My heart is leaning on the Word,
  Am **G**   **D** **G**
The living Word of God:
    G   **C**
Salvation by my Savior's name,
  Am **G**   **D** **G**
Salvation through His blood.

Verse 4
     G   **C**
My great Physician heals the sick,
  Am **G**   **D** **G**
The lost He came to save;
    G   **C**
For me His precious blood He shed,
  Am **G**   **D** **G**
For me His life He gave.

My Jesus, I Love Thee

Words by WILLIAM R. FEATHERSTON
Music by ADONIRAM J. GORDON

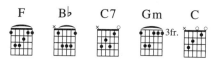

Verse 1

      F B♭ F   C7   F
My Je- sus, I love Thee, I know Thou art mine;
    F B♭ F   C7   F
For Thee all the follies of sin I resign.
   F B♭ F C7   F Gm F C
My gracious Re-deemer, my Sav-ior art Thou:
  F B♭ F   C7   F
If ev- er I loved Thee, my Jesus, 'tis now.

Verse 2

    F B♭   F   C7   F
I love Thee because Thou hast first loved me
     F B♭   F   C7   F
And pur-chased my pardon on Calvary's tree.
   F B♭   F C7   F Gm F C
I love Thee for wearing the thorns on Thy brow:
  F B♭ F   C7   F
If ev- er I loved Thee, my Jesus, 'tis now.

Arr. © Copyright 2010 Universal Music - Brentwood-Benson Publishing (ASCAP)
(Licensing through Music Services). All rights reserved. Used by permission.

Verse 3

      F   B♭   F   C7   F
I'll love Thee in life, I will love Thee in death,
     F   B♭   F   C7   F
And praise Thee as long as Thou lendest me breath.
       F   B♭   F C7   F   Gm   F C
And say, when the death dew lies cold on my brow,
      F   B♭ F   C7   F
"If ev- er I loved Thee, my Jesus, 'tis now."

Verse 4

      F   B♭   F   C7   F
In mansions of glory and endless delight,
     F   B♭   F   C7   F
I'll ev- er adore Thee in heaven so bright.
      F   B♭   F C7   F   Gm   F C
I'll sing with the glittering crown on my brow;
      F   B♭ F   C7   F
"If ev- er I loved Thee, my Jesus, 'tis now."

No, Not One

Words by JOHNSON OATMAN, JR.
Music by GEORGE C. HUGG

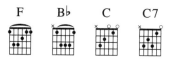

Verse 1   F   B♭   F
There's not a friend like the lowly Jesus,
             F   C   F   C7   F
No, not one! No, not   one!
             F   B♭   F
None else could heal all our soul's diseases,
             F   C   F   C7   F
No, not one! No, not   one!

Chorus   F   C7   F
Jesus knows all about our struggles;
             F   C
He will guide till the day is done.
             F   B♭   F
There's not a friend like the lowly Jesus,
             F   C   F   C7   F
No, not one! No, not   one!

Arr. © Copyright 2010 Universal Music - Brentwood-Benson Publishing (ASCAP)
(Licensing through Music Services). All rights reserved. Used by permission.

Verse 2
    F   B♭   F
No friend like Him is so high and holy,
F   C   F   C7 F
No, not one! No, not   one!
F   B♭   F
And yet no friend is so meek and lowly,
F   C   F   C7 F
No, not one! No, not   one!

Verse 3
    F   B♭ F
There's not an hour that He is not near us,
F   C   F   C7 F
No, not one! No, not   one!
F   B♭   F
No night so dark but His love can cheer us,
F   C   F   C7 F
No, not one! No, not   one!

Verse 4
    F   B♭   F
Did ever saint find this friend forsake him?
F   C   F   C7 F
No, not one! No, not   one!
F   B♭   F
Or sinner find that He would not take him?
F   C   F   C7 F
No, not one! No, not   one!

Verse 5
    F   B♭   F
Was e'er a gift like the Savior given?
F   C   F   C7 F
No, not one! No, not   one!
F   B♭   F
Will He refuse us a home in heaven?
F   C   F   C7 F
No, not one! No, not   one!

Nothing but the Blood

Words and Music by
ROBERT LOWRY

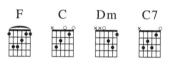

Verse 1
    F   C F
What can wash a- way my sin?
    F   Dm   C7 F
Nothing but the blood of Je- sus;
    F   C F
What can make me whole again?
    F   Dm   C7 F
Nothing but the blood of Je- sus.

Chorus
    F   C F
Oh! precious is the flow
    C7   F
That makes me white as snow;
    F   C F
No other fount I know,
    F   Dm   C7 F
Nothing but the blood of Je- sus.

Arr. © Copyright 2010 Universal Music - Brentwood-Benson Publishing (ASCAP)
(Licensing through Music Services). All rights reserved. Used by permission.

Verse 2
```
F           C   F
```
For my pardon this I see,
```
F              Dm      C7   F
```
Nothing but the blood of Je- sus;
```
F           C   F
```
For my cleansing, this my plea,
```
F              Dm      C7   F
```
Nothing but the blood of Je- sus.

Verse 3
```
F           C   F
```
Nothing can for sin atone,
```
F              Dm      C7   F
```
Nothing but the blood of Je- sus;
```
F              C   F
```
Naught of good that I have done,
```
F              Dm      C7   F
```
Nothing but the blood of Je- sus.

Verse 4
```
F      C   F
```
This is all my hope and peace,
```
F              Dm      C7   F
```
Nothing but the blood of Je- sus;
```
F         C   F
```
This is all my righteousness,
```
F              Dm      C7   F
```
Nothing but the blood of Je- sus.

O for a Thousand Tongues to Sing

Words by CHARLES WESLEY
Music by CARL G. GLÄSER

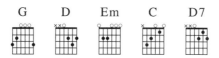

Verse 1
        G   **D**   **G**   **Em**
O for a thousand tongues to sing
D **G**   **C** **G** **D**
My great Redeemer's praise,
      G   **C**
The glories of my God and King,
      G   **D7** **G**
The triumphs of His grace!

Verse 2
        G   **D**   **G**   **Em**
My gracious Master and my God,
D **G**   **C** **G** **D**
As- sist me to pro- claim,
      G   **C**
To spread through all the earth abroad
      G   **D7** **G**
The honors of Thy name.

Arr. © Copyright 2010 Universal Music - Brentwood-Benson Publishing (ASCAP)
(Licensing through Music Services). All rights reserved. Used by permission.

Verse 3

      G   D   G   Em
Jesus, the name that calms my fears,
D G   C G D
That bids my sor- rows cease;
     G   C
'Tis music in the sinner's ears;
     G   D7 G
'Tis life and health and peace.

Verse 4

      G   D   G   Em
He breaks the power of cancelled sin,
D G   C G D
He sets the prisoner free;
     G   C
His blood can make the foulest clean,
     G   D7 G
His blood availed for me.

O Worship the King
Words by ROBERT GRANT
Music by JOHANN M. HAYDN

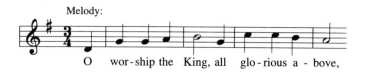

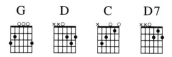

Verse 1

     G   D G   C   G   D
O worship the King, all glorious a- bove,
     G   D G C G   D G
And gratefully sing His wonderful love;
     D   D7
Our Shield and Defender, the Ancient of Days,
     G   D G   C G   D   G
Pavilioned in splendor, and girded with praise.

Verse 2

     G   D G   C   G   D
O tell of His might, O sing of His grace,
     G   D G   C   G D G
Whose robe is the light, whose canopy space!
     D   D7
His chariots of wrath the deep thunderclouds form,
     G   D G   C G   D G
And dark is His path on the wings of the storm.

Arr. © Copyright 2010 Universal Music - Brentwood-Benson Publishing (ASCAP)
(Licensing through Music Services). All rights reserved. Used by permission.

Verse 3

      G   D G   C   G D
Thy bountiful care what tongue can re- cite?
  G   D G C G   D G
It breathes in the air, it shines in the light;
  D   D7
It streams from the hills, it descends to the plain,
    G   D G   C G   D G
And sweetly dis- tills in the dew and the rain.

Verse 4

     G   D G   C   G D
Frail children of dust, and feeble as frail,
  G   D G C G   D G
In Thee do we trust, nor find Thee to fail:
  D   D7
Thy mercies how tender, how firm to the end;
    G   D G   C G   D G
Our Maker, De- fender, Re- deemer, and Friend!

Oh, How I Love Jesus

Words by FREDERICK WHITFIELD
Music: Traditional

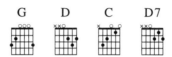

Verse 1   G
There is a name I love to hear,
     D   G
I love to sing its worth;
     G
It sounds as music in my ear,
     C   D   G
The sweetest name on earth.

Chorus   G
Oh, how I love Jesus,
   D7   G
Oh, how I love Jesus,
   G
Oh, how I love Jesus,
     C   D   G
Because He first loved me.

Arr. © Copyright 2010 Universal Music - Brentwood-Benson Publishing (ASCAP)
(Licensing through Music Services). All rights reserved. Used by permission.

Verse 2

```
       G
It tells me of a Savior's love,
       D           G
Who died to set me free;
       G
It tells me of His precious blood,
     C    D    G
The sinner's perfect plea.
```

Verse 3

```
       G
It tells me what my Father has
     D          G
In store for every day;
       G
And though I tread a darksome path,
     C    D     G
Yields sunshine all the way.
```

Verse 4

```
       G
It tells of One whose loving heart
       D           G
Can feel my deepest woe,
       G
Who in each sorrow bears a part
     C     D    G
That none can bear below.
```

Open My Eyes, That I May See

Words and Music by
CLARA H. SCOTT

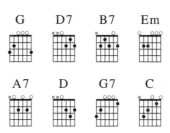

Verse 1

G	D7

Open my eyes, that I may see

D7   **G**
Glimpses of truth Thou hast for me;
B7   **Em**   **B7**   **Em**
Place in my hands the wonderful key
A7   **D**
That shall unclasp and set me free.
G   **D7**
Silently now I wait for Thee,
D7   **G**
Ready, my God, Thy will to see;
G   **G7**   **C**   **D7**   **G**
Open my eyes, illumine me, Spirit divine!

Arr. © Copyright 2010 Universal Music - Brentwood-Benson Publishing (ASCAP)
(Licensing through Music Services). All rights reserved. Used by permission.

Verse 2

```
G                    D7
Open my ears, that I may hear
D7                   G
Voices of truth Thou sendest clear;
B7          Em       B7        Em
And while the wave-notes fall on my ear,
A7                   D
Ev'rything false will disappear.
G          D7
Silently now I wait for Thee,
D7                   G
Ready, my God, Thy will to see;
G      G7    C        D7    G
Open my ears, illumine me, Spirit divine!
```

Verse 3

```
G                    D7
Open my mouth, and let me bear
D7                   G
Gladly the warm truth ev'rywhere;
B7         Em      B7       Em
Open my heart, and let me prepare
A7                        D
Love with Thy children, thus to share.
G          D7
Silently now I wait for Thee,
D7                   G
Ready, my God, Thy will to see;
G      G7    C        D7    G
Open my heart, illumine me, Spirit divine!
```

O How He Loves You and Me

Words and Music by
KURT KAISER

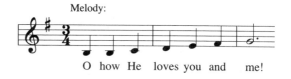

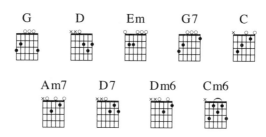

Verse 1	G D Em G7

O how He loves you and me!
C   Am7   D7   G
O how He loves you and   me!
G   Dm6   C   Cm6
He gave His life; what more could He give?
G   C   G   C
O how He loves you; O how He loves me;
G   Am7   D7   G
O how He loves you and   me!

Verse 2	G D Em G7

Jesus to Calvary did go;
C   Am7   D7   G
His love for sinners to   show.
G   Dm6   C   Cm6
What He did there brought hope from despair.
G   C   G   C
O how He loves you; O how He loves me;
G   Am7   D7   G
O how He loves you and   me!

© Copyright 1975 Word Music, LLC. All rights reserved. Used by permission.

Open Our Eyes, Lord

Words and Music by
BOB CULL

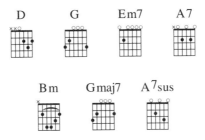

Chorus   **D**   **G**   **Em7**
                Open our eyes, Lord,
            A7   **G**   **D**   **Bm**
                We want to see Je- sus,
            Bm   **Gmaj7**   **Em7**   **A7sus**
                To reach out and touch   Him,
            A7   **G**   **D**
                And say that we love Him.
D   **G**   **Em7**
                Open our ears, Lord,
            A7   **G**   **D**   **Bm**
                And help us to lis- ten.
Bm   **Gmaj7**   **Em7**   **A7sus**
                Open our eyes,   Lord,
            A7   **D**
                We want to see Jesus.

© Copyright 1976 Maranatha Music / CCCM Music (ASCAP) (Administered by Music Services).
All rights reserved. Used by permission.

Praise Him! Praise Him!

Words by FANNY CROSBY
Music by CHESTER G. ALLEN

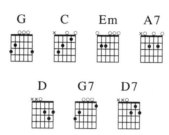

Verse 1
    G   C   G
Praise Him! praise Him! Jesus, our blessed Redeemer!
G   Em   A7   D
Sing, O earth, His wonderful love proclaim!
G   C   G
Hail Him! hail Him! highest archangels in glory,
G   G7 C   G   D7 G
Strength and honor give to His holy name!
D   G   D
Like a shepherd, Jesus will guard His children;
G   Em   A7   D
In His arms He carries them all day long.

Chorus
    G   C   G
Praise Him! praise Him! Tell of His excellent greatness!
G   G7 C   G   D7 G
Praise Him! praise Him! Ever in joyful song!

Arr. © Copyright 2010 Universal Music - Brentwood-Benson Publishing (ASCAP)
(Licensing through Music Services). All rights reserved. Used by permission.

Verse 2

G			C		G

Praise Him! praise Him! Jesus, our blessed Redeemer!

G	Em	A7		D

For our sins He suffered and bled and died;

G		C		G

He our Rock, our hope of eternal salvation,

G	G7	C	G	D7	G

Hail Him! hail Him! Jesus the crucified.

D		G	D

Sound His praises! Jesus who bore our sorrows,

G	Em	A7		D

Love unbounded, wonderful, deep, and strong!

Verse 3

G			C		G

Praise Him! praise Him! Jesus, our blessed Redeemer!

G	Em	A7		D

Heav'nly portals loud with hosannas ring!

G		C		G

Jesus, Savior, reigneth forever and ever;

G	G7	C	G	D7	G

Crown Him! Crown Him! Prophet and Priest and King!

D		G	D

Christ is coming, over the world victorious;

G	Em	A7		D

Power and glory unto the Lord belong!

Praise to the Lord, the Almighty

Words by JOACHIM NEANDER
Music: German Hymn

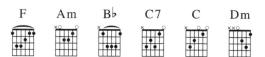

Verse 1
    F   Am
Praise to the Lord, the Almighty,
    B♭   C7   F
The King of crea- tion!
F
O my soul, praise Him,
    Am   B♭   C7   F
For He is thy health and salva- tion!
F   B♭   F   C
All ye who hear, Now to His temple draw near;
F   Dm   C7   F
Praise Him in glad adora- tion!

Verse 2
    F   Am
Praise to the Lord, who o'er all things
    B♭   C7   F
So wondrously reigneth,
F   Am
Shelters thee under His wings,
    B♭   C7   F
Yea, so gently sustain- eth!
F   B♭   F   C
Hast thou not seen How thy desires e'er have been
F   Dm   C7   F
Granted in what He ordain- eth?

Arr. © Copyright 2010 Universal Music - Brentwood-Benson Publishing (ASCAP)
(Licensing through Music Services). All rights reserved. Used by permission.

Verse 3

```
     F                        Am
Praise to the Lord, who doth prosper
       Bb       C7   F
Thy work and defend  thee;
     F                      Am
Surely His goodness and mercy
       Bb      C7   F
Here daily attend  thee.
     F      Bb   F                 C
Ponder anew What the Almighty can do
     F         Dm       C7   F
If with His love He befriend thee.
```

Verse 4

```
     F                     Am
Praise to the Lord, O let all that
       Bb     C7   F
Is in me adore  Him!
     F
All that hath life and breath,
     Am           Bb      C7   F
Come now with praises before  Him.
     F       Bb  F                    C
Let the Amen Sound from His people again;
     F         Dm      C7    F
Gladly for aye we adore  Him!
```

Take My Hand, Precious Lord

Words and Music by
THOMAS A. DORSEY

Verse 1
      G   G7
Precious Lord, take my hand.
  C
Lead me on, help me stand–
    G   Em   D A7 D
I am tired, I am weak, I am worn;
    G   G7
Thro' the storm, thro' the night,
    C
Lead me on to the light–
    G   D7   G C G
Take my hand, precious Lord, lead me home.

Verse 2
      G   G7
When my way grows drear,
  C
Precious Lord, linger near–
    G   Em D A7 D
When my life is almost gone;
    G   G7
Hear my cry, hear my call,
  C
Hold my hand lest I fall–
    G   D7   G C G
Take my hand, precious Lord, lead me home.

© Copyright 1938 (Renewed) Warner-Tamerlane Publishing Corp.
All rights reserved. Used by permission.

Rejoice in the Lord Always

Traditional

Chorus
        F   **C7**   **F**
Rejoice in the Lord always: again I say, rejoice!
        F   **C7**   **F**
Rejoice in the Lord always: again I say, rejoice!
        F   **C7**   **F**
Rejoice, rejoice, and again I say, rejoice!
        F   **C7**   **F**
Rejoice, rejoice, and again I say, rejoice!
        F   **C7**   **F**
Rejoice in the Lord always: again I say, rejoice!
        F   **C7**   **F**
Rejoice in the Lord always: again I say, rejoice!

Arr. © Copyright 2010 Universal Music - Brentwood-Benson Publishing (ASCAP)
(Licensing through Music Services). All rights reserved. Used by permission.

Rock of Ages, Cleft for Me

Words by AUGUSTUS M. TOPLADY
Music by THOMAS HASTINGS

Melody:

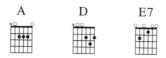

Rock of A - ges, cleft for me,

```
   A         D         E7
```

Verse 1

     A   D   A
Rock of Ages, cleft for me,
     A   E7   A
Let me hide myself in Thee;
  E7   A
Let the water and the blood,
     E7   A
From Thy wounded side which flowed,
  A   D   A
Be of sin the double cure,
   A   E7   A
Save from wrath and make me pure.

Arr. © Copyright 2010 Universal Music - Brentwood-Benson Publishing (ASCAP)
(Licensing through Music Services). All rights reserved. Used by permission.

Verse 2

    A **D** **A**
Not the labors of my hands
   A **E7** **A**
Can fulfill Thy law's demands;
   E7   **A**
These for sin could not atone;
    E7   **A**
Thou must save, and Thou alone:
  A   **D** **A**
In my hand no price I bring,
   A **E7** **A**
Simply to Thy cross I cling.

Verse 3

    A   **D** **A**
While I draw this fleeting breath,
     A   **E7** **A**
When mine eyes shall close in death,
   E7   **A**
When I rise to worlds unknown,
   E7   **A**
And behold Thee on Thy throne,
  A **D** **A**
Rock of Ages, cleft for me,
  A **E7** **A**
Let me hide myself in Thee.

Savior, Like a Shepherd Lead Us

Words by DOROTHY A. THRUPP
Music by WILLIAM B. BRADBURY

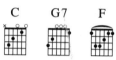

Verse 1   **C**
Savior, like a shepherd lead us,
G7   **C**
Much we need Thy tender care;
C
In Thy pleasant pastures feed us,
G7   **C**
For our use Thy folds prepare:
       F   **C**
Blessed Jesus, blessed Jesus,
           G7   **C**
Thou hast bought us, Thine we are;
       F   **C**
Blessed Jesus, blessed Jesus,
        C   **G7**   **C**
Thou hast bought us, Thine we are.

Verse 2   **C**
We are Thine; do Thou befriend us,
G7   **C**
Be the guardian of our way;
C
Keep Thy flock, from sin defend us,
G7   **C**
Seek us when we go astray:
       F   **C**   **G7**   **C**
Blessed Jesus, blessed Jesus, Hear, O hear us when we pray;
       F   **C**   **G7**   **C**
Blessed Jesus, blessed Jesus, Hear, O hear us when we pray.

Arr. © Copyright 2010 Universal Music - Brentwood-Benson Publishing (ASCAP)
(Licensing through Music Services). All rights reserved. Used by permission.

Verse 3

C
Thou hast promised to receive us,
G7   C
Poor and sinful though we be;
C
Thou hast mercy to relieve us,
G7   C
Grace to cleanse and power to free:
   F   C
Blessed Jesus, blessed Jesus,
  G7 C
Early let us turn to Thee;
   F   C
Blessed Jesus, blessed Jesus,
 C G7 C
Early let us turn to Thee.

Verse 4

C
Early let us seek Thy favor;
G7   C
Early let us do Thy will;
C
Blessed Lord and only Savior,
G7   C
With Thy love our beings fill:
   F   C
Blessed Jesus, blessed Jesus,
   G7   C
Thou hast loved us, love us still;
   F   C
Blessed Jesus, blessed Jesus,
   C G7 C
Thou hast loved us, love us still.

Shall We Gather at the River?

Words and Music by
ROBERT LOWRY

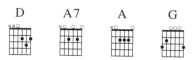

Verse 1

D
Shall we gather at the river,
A7
Where bright angel feet have trod;
D
With its crystal tide forever
    A   A7   D
Flowing from the throne of God?

Chorus

G   D
Yes, we'll gather at the river,
  A7   D
The beautiful, the beautiful river;
G   D
Gather with the saints at the river
  A   A7   D
That flows from the throne of God.

Arr. © Copyright 2010 Universal Music - Brentwood-Benson Publishing (ASCAP)
(Licensing through Music Services). All rights reserved. Used by permission.

Verse 2
D
On the margin of the river,
A7
Washing up its silver spray,
D
We will walk and worship ever,
    A   **A7**   **D**
All the happy golden day.

Verse 3
D
Ere we reach the shining river,
A7
Lay we every burden down;
D
Grace our spirits will deliver,
    A   **A7**   **D**
And provide a robe and crown.

Verse 4
D
Soon we'll reach the shining river,
A7
Soon our pilgrimage will cease;
D
Soon our happy hearts will quiver
   A **A7** **D**
With the melody of peace.

Since Jesus Came into My Heart

Words by RUFUS H. McDANIEL
Music by CHARLES H. GABRIEL

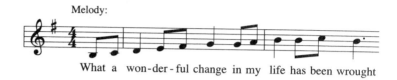

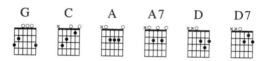

Verse 1
        G
What a wonderful change in my life has been wrought
  C   G
Since Jesus came into my heart!
      G
I have light in my soul for which long I had sought,
  A   A7   D D7
Since Jesus came into my heart!

Chorus
       G
Since Jesus came into my heart,
  C   G
Since Jesus came into my heart,
      G
Floods of joy o'er my soul like the sea billows roll,
 C   G   D7   G
Since Jesus came into my heart!

Arr. © Copyright 2010 Universal Music - Brentwood-Benson Publishing (ASCAP)
(Licensing through Music Services). All rights reserved. Used by permission.

Verse 2

        G
I'm possessed of a hope that is steadfast and sure,
   C   G
Since Jesus came into my heart!
        G
And no dark clouds of doubt now my pathway obscure,
  A   A7   D   D7
Since Jesus came into my heart!

Verse 3

      G
There's a light in the valley of death now for me,
   C   G
Since Jesus came into my heart!
      G
And the gates of the city beyond I can see,
  A   A7   D   D7
Since Jesus came into my heart!

Verse 4

     G
I shall go there to dwell in that city, I know,
   C   G
Since Jesus came into my heart!
     G
And I'm happy, so happy, as onward I go,
  A   A7   D   D7
Since Jesus came into my heart!

Softly and Tenderly

Words and Music by
WILL L. THOMPSON

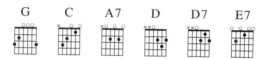

Verse 1
    G   C   G
Softly and tenderly Jesus is calling,
G   A7   D D7
Calling for you and for me;
G   C   G
See, on the portals He's waiting and watching,
G   C G   D7   G
Watching for you and for me.

Chorus
        D7   G D G
Come home, come home,
D   E7   A7   D A7 D7
Ye who are weary come home;
G   C   G
Earnestly, tenderly, Jesus is calling,
G   C G   D7   G
Calling, O sinner, come home!

Arr. © Copyright 2010 Universal Music - Brentwood-Benson Publishing (ASCAP)
(Licensing through Music Services). All rights reserved. Used by permission.

Verse 2

```
        G                       C       G
Why should we tarry when Jesus is pleading,
        G        A7       D   D7
Pleading for you and for me?
        G                  C         G
Why should we linger and heed not His mercies,
        G     C   G      D7   G
Mercies for you and for   me?
```

Verse 3

```
        G                   C         G
Time is now fleeting, the moments are passing,
        G        A7       D   D7
Passing from you and from me;
        G                  C         G
Shadows are gathering, deathbeds are coming,
        G     C   G      D7   G
Coming for you and for   me.
```

Verse 4

```
        G                  C         G
Oh! for the wonderful love He has promised,
        G        A7       D   D7
Promised for you and for me;
        G                         C         G
Though we have sinned He has mercy and pardon,
        G     C   G      D7   G
Pardon for you and for   me.
```

TOP 100 HYMNS

Standing on the Promises

Words and Music by
R. KELSO CARTER

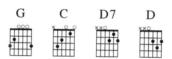

Verse 1   G
Standing on the promises of Christ, my King,
  C   G
Through eternal ages let His praises ring;
  G
"Glory in the highest," I will shout and sing,
  G   D7   G
Standing on the promises of God.

Chorus   G   C
Standing, standing,
  D   G
Standing on the promises of God my Savior;
  G   C
Standing, standing,
        G   D7   G
I'm standing on the promises of God.

Arr. © Copyright 2010 Universal Music - Brentwood-Benson Publishing (ASCAP)
(Licensing through Music Services). All rights reserved. Used by permission.

Verse 2   **G**
Standing on the promises that cannot fail,
C   **G**
When the howling storms of doubt and fear assail,
G
By the living Word of God I shall prevail,
G   **D7**   **G**
Standing on the promises of God.

Verse 3   **G**
Standing on the promises of Christ, the Lord,
C   **G**
Bound to Him eternally by love's strong cord,
G
Overcoming daily with the Spirit's sword,
G   **D7**   **G**
Standing on the promises of God.

Verse 4   **G**
Standing on the promises I cannot fall,
C   **G**
List'ning every moment to the Spirit's call,
G
Resting in my Savior as my all in all,
G   **D7**   **G**
Standing on the promises of God.

Sweet Hour of Prayer

Words by WILLIAM W. WALFORD
Music by WILLIAM B. BRADBURY

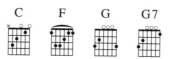

Verse 1

        C   F
Sweet hour of prayer, sweet hour of prayer,
    C   G
That calls me from a world of care
    C   F
And bids me at my Father's throne
    C   G7 C
Make all my wants and wishes   known!
    C
In seasons of distress and grief
    C   G
My soul has often found relief,
    C   F
And oft escaped the tempter's snare
    C   G7 C
By thy return, sweet hour of   prayer.

Arr. © Copyright 2010 Universal Music - Brentwood-Benson Publishing (ASCAP)
(Licensing through Music Services). All rights reserved. Used by permission.

Verse 2

     C   F
Sweet hour of prayer, sweet hour of prayer,
    C   G
Thy wings shall my petition bear
  C   F
To Him whose truth and faithfulness
    C   G7 C
Engage the waiting soul to bless:
   C
And since He bids me seek His face,
    C   G
Believe His Word and trust His grace,
   C   F
I'll cast on Him my every care,
     C   G7 C
And wait for thee, sweet hour of prayer.

Verse 3

     C   F
Sweet hour of prayer, sweet hour of prayer,
   C   G
May I thy consolation share,
    C   F
Till, from Mount Pisgah's lofty height,
    C   G7 C
I view my home and take my flight:
    C
This robe of flesh I'll drop and rise
    C   G
To seize the everlasting prize;
     C   F
And shout, while passing through the air,
     C   G7 C
"Farewell, farewell, sweet hour of prayer!"

Take My Life, and Let It Be Consecrated

Words by FRANCES R. HAVERGAL
Music by HENRI A. CÉSAR MALAN

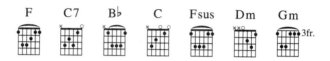

Verse 1

F   C7 F
Take my life and let it be
F   Bb   F   C7 F
Consecrated, Lord, to Thee;
F   C   C7   Fsus F
Take my hands and let them move
F   Bb F C F   C
At the im- pulse of Thy love,
Dm C F **Gm** F C F
At the im- pulse of Thy love.

Verse 2

F   C7   F
Take my feet and let them be
F   Bb   F C7 F
Swift and beautiful for Thee;
F   C   C7   Fsus F
Take my voice and let me sing
F   Bb F C F   C
Always, on- ly, for my King,
Dm C   F **Gm** F C F
Al- ways, on- ly, for my King.

Verse 3

```
        F              C7      F
        Take my silver and my gold,
        F     B♭       F   C7   F
        Not a mite would I  with- hold;
        F        C         C7      Fsus   F
        Take my moments and my days,
        F       B♭  F   C   F           C
        Let them flow in  ceaseless praise,
        Dm   C   F   Gm   F    C   F
        Let  them flow in   ceaseless praise.
```

Verse 4

```
        F              C7      F
        Take my will and make it Thine,
        F     B♭       F   C7   F
        It shall be no longer   mine;
        F        C         C7      Fsus   F
        Take my heart, it is Thine own,
        F      B♭   F   C   F   C
        It shall be  Thy roy- al  throne,
        Dm   C   F   Gm   F   C   F
        It   shall be  Thy roy- al  throne.
```

The Old Rugged Cross

Words and Music by
GEORGE BENNARD

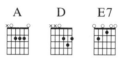

Verse 1
      A   D
On a hill far away stood an old rugged cross,
    E7   A
The emblem of suff'ring and shame;
    A   D
And I love that old cross where the dearest and best
    E7   A
For a world of lost sinners was slain.

Chorus
    E7   A
So I'll cherish the old rugged cross,
    D   A
Till my trophies at last I lay down;
    A   D
I will cling to the old rugged cross,
    A   E7   A
And exchange it someday for a crown.

Verse 2

     A   D
Oh, that old rugged cross, so despised by the world,
  E7   A
Has a wondrous attraction for me;
   A   D
For the dear Lamb of God left His glory above
 E7   A
To bear it to dark Calvary.

Verse 3

   A   D
In the old rugged cross, stained with blood so divine,
  E7   A
Such a wonderful beauty I see;
   A   D
For 'twas on that old cross Jesus suffered and died
 E7   A
To pardon and sanctify me.

Verse 4

   A   D
To the old rugged cross I will ever be true;
 E7   A
Its shame and reproach gladly bear.
   A   D
Then He'll call me some day to my home far away,
  E7   A
Where His glory forever I'll share.

The Solid Rock (My Hope Is Built)
Words by EDWARD MOTE
Music by WILLIAM B. BRADBURY

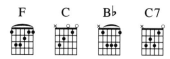

Verse 1
       F   C
My hope is built on nothing less
    B♭   C   F
Than Jesus' blood and righteousness;
  F   C
I dare not trust the sweetest frame,
    B♭   C   F
But wholly lean on Jesus' name.

Chorus
     F   B♭
On Christ, the solid Rock, I stand;
    F   C
All other ground is sinking sand,
  F   B♭ F C7   F
All other ground is   sinking sand.

Arr. © Copyright 2010 Universal Music - Brentwood-Benson Publishing (ASCAP)
(Licensing through Music Services). All rights reserved. Used by permission.

Verse 2
        F   C
When darkness seems to hide His face,
  B♭   C   F
I rest on His unchanging grace;
     F   C
In every high and stormy gale,
  B♭   C F
My anchor holds within the veil.

Verse 3
     F   C
His oath, His covenant, His blood
  B♭   C   F
Support me in the whelming flood;
     F   C
When all around my soul gives way,
  B♭   C   F
He then is all my hope and stay.

Verse 4
     F   C
When He shall come with trumpet sound,
  B♭   C   F
Oh, may I then in Him be found;
      F   C
Dressed in His righteousness alone,
  B♭   C   F
Faultless to stand before the throne.

There Is a Fountain

Words by WILLIAM COWPER
Music: Traditional

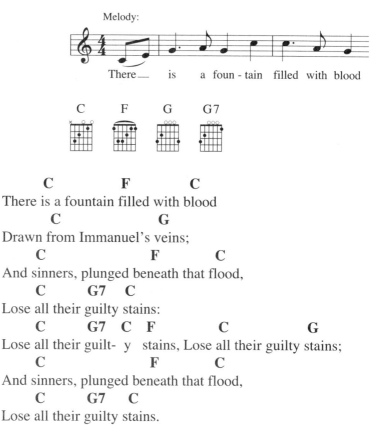

Verse 1
      C   F   C
There is a fountain filled with blood
      C   G
Drawn from Immanuel's veins;
      C   F   C
And sinners, plunged beneath that flood,
    C   G7 C
Lose all their guilty stains:
    C   G7 C F   C   G
Lose all their guilt- y stains, Lose all their guilty stains;
      C   F   C
And sinners, plunged beneath that flood,
    C   G7 C
Lose all their guilty stains.

Verse 2
      C   F   C
The dying thief rejoiced to see
      C   G
That fountain in his day;
      C   F C   G7 C
And there may I, though vile as he, Wash all my sins away:
    C   G7 C F   C   G
Wash all my sins a- way, Wash all my sins away;
      C   F C   G7 C
And there may I, though vile as he, Wash all my sins away.

Arr. © Copyright 2010 Universal Music - Brentwood-Benson Publishing (ASCAP)
(Licensing through Music Services). All rights reserved. Used by permission.

Verse 3

    C   F   C
Dear dying Lamb, Thy precious blood
    C   G
Shall never lose its power
    C   F   C
Till all the ransomed church of God
    C   G7 C
Be saved, to sin no more:
    C   G7 C F   C   G
Be saved, to sin no more, Be saved, to sin no more;
    C   F   C
Till all the ransomed church of God
    C   G7 C
Be saved, to sin no more.

Verse 4

    C   F   C
E'er since by faith I saw the stream
    C   G
Thy flowing wounds supply,
    C   F   C   G7 C
Redeeming love has been my theme, And shall be till I die:
     C   G7 C F   C   G
And shall be till I die, And shall be till I die;
    C   F   C   G7 C
Redeeming love has been my theme, And shall be till I die.

Verse 5

    C   F   C
When this poor lisping, stamm'ring tongue
    C   G
Lies silent in the grave,
    C   F   C   G7   C
Then in a nobler, sweeter song, I'll sing Thy pow'r to save:
    C   G7 C F   C   G
I'll sing Thy pow'r to save, I'll sing Thy pow'r to save;
    C   F   C   G7   C
Then in a nobler, sweeter song, I'll sing Thy pow'r to save.

There Is Power in the Blood

Words and Music by
LEWIS E. JONES

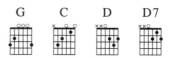

Verse 1
    G   C   G
Would you be free from the burden of sin?
            D   G
There's power in the blood, power in the blood;
G   C   G
Would you o'er evil a victory win?
            D   D7   G
There's wonderful power in the blood.

Chorus
          G   C   G
There is power, power, wonder-working power
    D7   G
In the blood of the Lamb.
          G   C   G
There is power, power, wonder-working power
   D   D7   G
In the precious blood of the Lamb.

Arr. © Copyright 2010 Universal Music - Brentwood-Benson Publishing (ASCAP)
(Licensing through Music Services). All rights reserved. Used by permission.

Verse 2

G   C   G
Would you be free from your passion and pride?
               D   G
There's power in the blood, power in the blood;
G   C   G
Come for a cleansing to Calvary's tide;
           D   D7   G
There's wonderful power in the blood.

Verse 3

G   C   G
Would you be whiter, much whiter than snow?
              D   G
There's power in the blood, power in the blood;
G   C   G
Sin stains are lost in its lifegiving flow;
          D   D7   G
There's wonderful power in the blood.

Verse 4

G   C   G
Would you do service for Jesus your King?
             D   G
There's power in the blood, power in the blood;
G   C   G
Would you live daily His praises to sing?
          D   D7   G
There's wonderful power in the blood.

'Tis So Sweet to Trust in Jesus

Words by LOUISA M. R. STEAD
Music by WILLIAM J. KIRKPATRICK

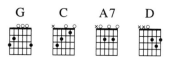

Verse 1

    G   C   G
'Tis so sweet to trust in Jesus,
G   A7   D
Just to take Him at His word;
G   C   G
Just to rest upon His promise,
G   C   G   D   G
Just to know, "Thus saith the Lord."

Chorus

G   D   G   D
Jesus, Jesus, how I trust Him!
G   A7   D
How I've proved Him o'er and o'er!
G   C   G
Jesus, Jesus, precious Jesus!
G   C   G   D   G
O for grace to trust Him more!

Arr. © Copyright 2010 Universal Music - Brentwood-Benson Publishing (ASCAP)
(Licensing through Music Services). All rights reserved. Used by permission.

Verse 2
```
         G              C      G
         O how sweet to trust in Jesus,
         G              A7     D
         Just to trust His cleansing blood;
         G              C      G
         Just in simple faith to plunge me
          G      C       G  D  G
         'Neath the healing, cleansing  flood!
```

Verse 3
```
         G              C      G
         Yes, 'tis sweet to trust in Jesus,
         G              A7  D
         Just from sin and self to cease;
         G              C      G
         Just from Jesus simply taking
         G      C       G  D  G
         Life and rest, and joy and peace.
```

Verse 4
```
         G              C      G
         I'm so glad I learned to trust Him,
         G              A7  D
         Precious Jesus, Savior, Friend;
         G              C      G
         And I know that He is with me,
         G      C       G  D  G
         Will be with me to   the end.
```

To God Be the Glory

Words by FANNY CROSBY
Music by WILLIAM H. DOANE

Melody: To God be the glo-ry, great things He hath done;

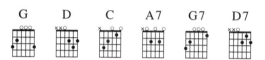

G   D   C   A7   G7   D7

Verse 1
    G   D   G
To God be the glory, great things He hath done;
  C   G   A7   D
So loved He the world that He gave us His Son,
    G   D   G7
Who yielded His life an atonement for sin,
  C   G   D7 G
And opened the lifegate that all may go   in.

Chorus
        G   D
Praise the Lord, praise the Lord, Let the earth hear His voice!
  D7   G   D7 G
Praise the Lord, praise the Lord, Let the people re-   joice!
  G   D   G7
O come to the Father through Jesus, the Son,
  C   G   D7 G
And give Him the glory, great things He hath done!

Arr. © Copyright 2010 Universal Music - Brentwood-Benson Publishing (ASCAP)
(Licensing through Music Services). All rights reserved. Used by permission.

Verse 2
```
            G                    D           G
       O perfect redemption, the purchase of blood,
            C       G        A7       D
       To every believer the promise of God;
            G                D        G7
       The vilest offender who truly believes,
            C             G           D7   G
       That moment from Jesus a pardon re-  ceives.
```

Verse 3
```
                  G                     D            G
       Great things He hath taught us, great things He hath done,
            C       G          A7       D
       And great our rejoicing through Jesus the Son;
            G                 D         G7
       But purer, and higher, and greater will be
            C          G              D7   G
       Our wonder, our vict'ry, when Jesus we  see.
```

Trust and Obey

Words by JOHN H. SAMMIS
Music by DANIEL B. TOWNER

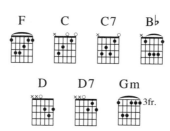

Verse 1
        F   C   F
When we walk with the Lord
   C   C7 F
In the light of His Word,
 B♭   F   C
What a glory He sheds on our way!
      F   C   F
Let us do His good will;
   C   C7 F
He abides with us still,
  B♭   F   C F
And with all who will trust and o- bey.

Chorus C   F   D D7 Gm
Trust and obey, For there's no other way
   C7   F   C F
To be happy in Jesus, But to trust and o- bey.

Arr. © Copyright 2010 Universal Music - Brentwood-Benson Publishing (ASCAP)
(Licensing through Music Services). All rights reserved. Used by permission.

Verse 2

      F   C F
Not a burden we bear,
  C   C7 F
Not a sorrow we share,
    B♭   F   C
But our toil He doth richly repay;
   F   C   F
Not a grief or a loss,
   C   C7 F
Not a frown or a cross
   B♭   F   C F
But is blest if we trust and o- bey.

Verse 3

      F   C F
But we never can prove
    C   C7 F
The delights of His love
   B♭   F   C
Until all on the altar we lay;
    F   C F
For the favor He shows
    C   C7 F
And the joy He be- stows
   B♭   F   C F
Are for them who will trust and o- bey.

Verse 4

      F   C F
Then in fellowship sweet
   C   C7 F
We will sit at His feet,
    B♭   F   C
Or we'll walk by His side in the way;
     F   C F
What He says we will do,
    C   C7 F
Where He sends we will go;
   B♭   F   C F
Never fear, only trust and o- bey.

TOP 100 HYMNS

Turn Your Eyes Upon Jesus

Words and Music by
HELEN H. LEMMEL

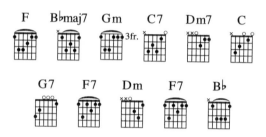

Verse 1
     F   B♭maj7 Gm
O soul, are you weary and trou-   bled?
   F   C7   F
No light in the darkness you see?
           F   Dm7 C
There's light for a look at the Sav- ior,
   F   C   G7   C
And life more abundant and free!

Chorus
   F   C   Dm   F7
Turn your eyes upon Je- sus,
 B♭   C7
Look full in His wonderful face,
      F   Dm F7 B♭
And the things of earth will grow strangely dim
   F   C7   F
In the light of His glory and grace.

Arr. © Copyright 2010 Universal Music - Brentwood-Benson Publishing (ASCAP)
(Licensing through Music Services). All rights reserved. Used by permission.

Verse 2

    F   B♭maj7 Gm
Through death into life everlast- ing
  F   C7   F
He passed, and we follow Him there;
  F   Dm7 C
O'er us sin no more hath domin- ion–
  F   C G7 C
For more than conq'rors we are!

Verse 3

    F   B♭maj7 Gm
His word shall not fail you– He prom- ised;
  F   C7   F
Believe Him, and all will be well.
  F   Dm7 C
Then go to a world that is dy- ing,
  F   C G7 C
His perfect salvation to tell!

Victory in Jesus

Words and Music by
E. M. BARTLETT

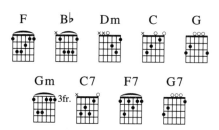

Verse 1

    F
I heard an old, old story,
  Bb   **F**
How a Savior came from glory,
     Dm   **C** **F**   **Dm**
How He gave His life on Calvary
  G   **C**
To save a wretch like me.
  F
I heard about His groaning,
  Bb   **F**
Of His precious blood's atoning,
    Dm   **C** **F**   **Dm**   **Gm**   **C7** **F**
Then I repented of my sins and won the victo-ry.

Chorus

     F   **F7**   **Bb**   **F**
O victory in Jesus, my Savior forever!
  Dm   **C** **F**   **G**   **G7**   **C**
He sought me and bought me with His redeeming blood;
    F   **F7**   **Bb**   **F**
He loved me ere I knew Him, and all my love is due Him.
    F   **C7**   **F**
He plunged me to victory, beneath the cleansing flood.

© Copyright 1939 by E.M. Bartlett. Copyright renewed 1966 by Mrs. E.M. Bartlett.
Assigned to Albert E. Brumley & Sons (SESAC) (Administered by EverGreen Copyrights).
All rights reserved. Used by permission.

Verse 2

       F
I heard about His healing,
    B♭   **F**
Of His cleansing power revealing,
    Dm   **C** **F**   **Dm**
How He made the lame to walk again
    G   **C**
And caused the blind to see.
    F
And then I cried, "Dear Jesus,
    B♭   **F**
Come and heal my broken spirit,"
  Dm   **C** **F**   **Dm**   **Gm** **C7** **F**
And somehow Jesus came and brought to me the victo-ry.

Verse 3

    F
I heard about a mansion
    B♭   **F**
He has built for me in glory,
  Dm   **C** **F**   **Dm**
And I heard about the streets of gold
  G   **C**
Beyond the crystal sea;
  F
About the angels singing,
  B♭   **F**
And the old redemption story,
  Dm   **C** **F**   **Dm**   **Gm** **C7** **F**
And some sweet day I'll sing up there the song of victo-ry.

Were You There?
Traditional

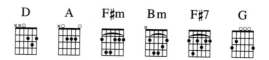

Verse 1
           D   A F#m   D
Were you there when they crucified my Lord?
       F#m   Bm D   A
Were you there when they cruci- fied my Lord?
D   A
Oh!
D   F#7 Bm   G   D   A
Sometimes it causes me to tremble, tremble, tremble.
         D   A F#m   D
Were you there when they crucified my Lord?

Verse 2
           D   A   F#m D
Were you there when they nailed Him to the tree?
       F#m   Bm   D   A
Were you there when they nailed Him to the tree?
D   A
Oh!
D   F#7 Bm   G   D   A
Sometimes it causes me to tremble, tremble, tremble.
         D   A   F#m D
Were you there when they nailed Him to the tree?

Arr. © Copyright 2010 Universal Music - Brentwood-Benson Publishing (ASCAP)
(Licensing through Music Services). All rights reserved. Used by permission.

Verse 3

     D   A F♯m D
Were you there when they laid Him in the tomb?
    F♯m   Bm   D A
Were you there when they laid Him in the tomb?
D A
Oh!
D   F♯7 Bm G   D   A
Sometimes it causes me to tremble, tremble, tremble.
     D   A F♯m D
Were you there when they laid Him in the tomb?

Verse 4

     D   A F♯m D
Were you there when He rose up from the grave?
    F♯m   Bm   D A
Were you there when He rose up from the grave?
D A
Oh!
D   F♯7 Bm G   D   A
Sometimes it causes me to tremble, tremble, tremble.
     D   A F♯m D
Were you there when He rose up from the grave?

What a Friend We Have in Jesus
Words by JOSEPH M. SCRIVEN
Music by CHARLES C. CONVERSE

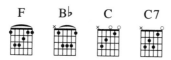

Verse 1
    F   B♭
What a friend we have in Jesus,
F   C
All our sins and griefs to bear!
F   B♭
What a privilege to carry
F   C7   F
Everything to God in prayer!
C   F
Oh, what peace we often forfeit,
B♭   F   C
Oh, what needless pain we bear,
F   B♭
All because we do not carry
F   C7   F
Everything to God in prayer!

Verse 2

```
F                         Bb
Have we trials and temptations?
F                   C
Is there trouble anywhere?
F                         Bb
We should never be discouraged;
F     C7         F
Take it to the Lord in prayer.
C                         F
Can we find a friend so faithful
Bb        F          C
Who will all our sorrows share?
F                         Bb
Jesus knows our ev'ry weakness,
F     C7         F
Take it to the Lord in prayer.
```

Verse 3

```
F                         Bb
Are we weak and heavy laden,
F                      C
Cumbered with a load of care?
F                         Bb
Precious Savior, still our refuge;
F     C7         F
Take it to the Lord in prayer.
C                         F
Do thy friends despise, forsake thee?
Bb       F           C
Take it to the Lord in prayer.
F                            Bb
In His arms He'll take and shield thee;
F     C7         F
Thou wilt find a solace there.
```

What Wondrous Love Is This
Traditional

Melody:

What wondrous love is this, O my soul, O my soul!

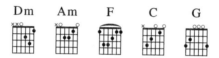

Verse 1   **Dm Am   F C   Dm   Am**
What wondrous love is this, O my soul, O my soul!
       Am   C   Dm
What wondrous love is this, O my soul!
G   Am   Dm   Am   Dm
What wondrous love is this that caused the Lord of bliss
    Dm   F C   Dm   Am
To bear the dreadful curse for my soul, for my soul,
    Am   F   G   Dm
To bear the dreadful curse for my soul.

Arr. © Copyright 2010 Universal Music - Brentwood-Benson Publishing (ASCAP)
(Licensing through Music Services). All rights reserved. Used by permission.

Verse 2
    Dm Am   F   C   Dm   Am
When I was sinking down, sinking down, sinking down,
       Am   C   Dm
When I was sinking down, sinking down,
  G   Am   Dm   Am   Dm
When I was sinking down beneath God's righteous frown,
     Dm   F   C   Dm   Am
Christ laid aside His crown for my soul, for my soul,
    Am   F   G   Dm
Christ laid aside His crown for my soul.

Verse 3
    Dm Am   F   C   Dm   Am
To God and to the Lamb, I will sing, I will sing;
    Am   C   Dm
To God and to the Lamb, I will sing.
G Am   Dm   Am   Dm
To God and to the Lamb Who is the great "I AM";
     Dm   F   C   Dm   Am
While millions join the theme, I will sing, I will sing;
    Am   F   G   Dm
While millions join the theme, I will sing.

Verse 4
    Dm Am   F   C   Dm   Am
And when from death I'm free, I'll sing on, I'll sing on;
    Am   C   Dm
And when from death I'm free, I'll sing on.
G Am   Dm   Am   Dm
And when from death I'm free, I'll sing and joyful be;
     Dm   F C   Dm   Am
And through eternity, I'll sing on, I'll sing on;
    Am   F G   Dm
And through eternity, I'll sing on.

When I Survey the Wondrous Cross
Words by ISAAC WATTS
Music by LOWELL MASON

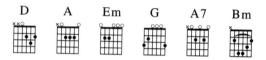

Verse 1
```
           D        A   D      Em   D  A   D
           When I sur- vey the won- drous   cross,
           D            G      D    A  A7  D   A
           On which the Prince of   Glory      died,
           D        A   D      Em   D  A   D
           My richest gain I count but    loss,
           D            A   Bm A    D  A7  D
           And pour contempt on  all my    pride.
```

Verse 2
```
           D        A   D      Em   D  A   D
           Forbid it, Lord, that I    should  boast,
           D            G      D    A  A7  D
           Save in the death of      Christ, my    God;
           D        A   D      Em   D  A   D
           All the vain things that charm me    most,
           D        A   Bm A    D  A7  D
           I sacrifice them to  His    blood.
```

Arr. © Copyright 2010 Universal Music - Brentwood-Benson Publishing (ASCAP)
(Licensing through Music Services). All rights reserved. Used by permission.

Verse 3

```
     D       A  D        Em    D  A  D
See, from His head, His hands, His    feet,
     D         G   D  A  D  A7 D  A
Sorrow and love flow    min-gled    down;
     D         A  D        Em    D  A  D
Did e'er such love and sor- row    meet,
     D            A  Bm   A  D  A7  D
Or thorns compose so   rich a      crown?
```

Verse 4

```
     D          A   D     Em    D  A  D
Were the whole realm of na- ture    mine,
     D          G  D  A  D  A7 D  A
That were a present   far too    small;
     D       A   D       Em   D  A  D
Love so a- mazing, so  di-    vine,
     D           A  Bm  A  D  A7  D
Demands my soul, my  life, my    all!
```

We'll Understand It Better By and By

Words and Music by
CHARLES A. TINDLEY

Melody: Tri - als dark on ev - 'ry hand, and we can - not un - der - stand

D G E7 A7

Verse 1

    D   G   D
Trials dark on every hand, and we cannot understand
  D
All the ways that God would lead us
    E7   A7
To that blessed promised land;
  D
But He'll guide us with His eye,
    G   D
And we'll follow till we die;
    D   A7   D
We will understand it better by and by.

Chorus

  D   G   D
By and by, when the morning comes,
  D   E7   A7
When the saints of God are gathered home,
    D   G   D
We will tell the story how we've overcome;
    D   A7   D
We will understand it better by and by.

Arr. © Copyright 2010 Universal Music - Brentwood-Benson Publishing (ASCAP)
(Licensing through Music Services). All rights reserved. Used by permission.

Verse 2

         D
Oft our cherished plans have failed,
    G   **D**
Disappointments have prevailed
          D
And we've wandered in the darkness,
  E7   **A7**
Heavy hearted and alone;
        D
But we're trusting in the Lord,
    G   **D**
And, according to His Word,
  D   **A7**   **D**
We will understand it better by and by.

Verse 3

  D   **G**   **D**
Temptations, hidden snares often take us unaware,
  D
And our hearts are made to bleed
  E7   **A7**
For some thoughtless word or deed,
  D
And we wonder why the test
  G   **D**
When we try to do our best,
  D   **A7**   **D**
But we'll understand it better by and by.

When the Roll Is Called Up Yonder

Words and Music by
JAMES M. BLACK

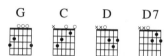

When the trum - pet of   the Lord shall sound,

G   C   D   D7

Verse 1
       G
When the trumpet of the Lord shall sound,
  C   G
And time shall be no more,
      G   D
And the morning breaks, eternal, bright, and fair;
     G
When the saved of earth shall gather over
C   G
On the other shore,
      G   D7   G
And the roll is called up yonder, I'll be there.

Chorus
     G
When the roll is called up yonder,
  D7
When the roll is called up yonder,
    G   C
When the roll is called up yonder,
    G   D7   G
When the roll is called up yonder, I'll be there.

Arr. © Copyright 2010 Universal Music - Brentwood-Benson Publishing (ASCAP)
(Licensing through Music Services). All rights reserved. Used by permission.

Verse 2

      G
On that bright and cloudless morning
      C   G
When the dead in Christ shall rise,
      G   D
And the glory of His resurrection share;
      G
When His chosen ones shall gather
      C   G
To their home beyond the skies,
      G   D7   G
And the roll is called up yonder, I'll be there.

Verse 3

      G
Let us labor for the Master
      C   G
From the dawn till setting sun,
      G   D
Let us talk of all His wondrous love and care;
      G
Then when all of life is over,
      C   G
And our work on earth is done,
      G   D7   G
And the roll is called up yonder, I'll be there.

When We All Get to Heaven

Words by ELIZA E. HEWITT
Music by EMILY D. WILSON

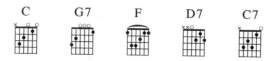

Sing the won-drous love— of— Je-sus,

Verse 1 C
Sing the wondrous love of Jesus,
G7   **C**
Sing His mercy and His grace;
C   **F**
In the mansions bright and blessed,
C   **G7**   **C F C**
He'll prepare for us a place.

Chorus   **C**
When we all get to heaven,
              C   **D7**   **G7**
What a day of rejoicing that will be!
              C C7 F
When we all   see Jesus,
              C   **G7**   **C F C**
We'll sing and shout the victory.

Arr. © Copyright 2010 Universal Music - Brentwood-Benson Publishing (ASCAP)
(Licensing through Music Services). All rights reserved. Used by permission.

Verse 2
C
While we walk the pilgrim pathway,
G7   C
Clouds will overspread the sky;
C   F
But when traveling days are over,
C   G7   C   F   C
Not a shadow, not a sigh.

Verse 3
C
Let us then be true and faithful,
G7   C
Trusting, serving every day;
C   F
Just one glimpse of Him in glory
C   G7   C   F   C
Will the toils of life repay.

Verse 4
C
Onward to the prize before us!
G7   C
Soon His beauty we'll behold;
C   F
Soon the pearly gates will open,
C   G7   C   F   C
We shall tread the streets of gold.

Revive Us Again

Words by WILLIAM P. MACKAY
Music by JOHN J. HUSBAND

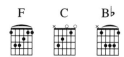

Verse 1
    F
We praise Thee, O God! for the Son of Thy love,
    F   **C**
For Jesus who died, and is now gone above.

Chorus
    B♭ **F**   **B♭** **F** **C**
Hallelu- jah! Thine the glory. Hallelu- jah! Amen.
    B♭ **F**   **B♭** **F** **C** **F**
Hallelu- jah! Thine the glory. Revive us a- gain.

Verse 2
    F
We praise Thee, O God! for Thy Spirit of light,
    F   **C**
Who hath shown us our Savior, and scattered our night.

Verse 3
    F
All glory and praise to the Lamb that was slain,
    F   **C**
Who hath borne all our sins, and hath cleansed every stain.

Verse 4
    F
Revive us again; fill each heart with Thy love;
    F   **C**
May each soul be rekindled with fire from above.

Arr. © Copyright 2010 Universal Music - Brentwood-Benson Publishing (ASCAP)
(Licensing through Music Services). All rights reserved. Used by permission.

A
A Mighty Fortress Is Our God —— 2
Abide with Me —— 4
All Creatures of Our God and King —— 6
All Hail the Power of Jesus' Name! —— 8
Amazing Grace! —— 10
And Can It Be —— 12
Are You Washed in the Blood? —— 14
At the Cross —— 16

B
Be Thou My Vision —— 18
Because He Lives —— 20
Bless the Lord, O My Soul —— 26
Blessed Assurance —— 22
Breathe on Me, Breath of God —— 24

C
Christ Arose —— 27
Christ the Lord Is Risen Today —— 28
Come, Thou Almighty King —— 30
Come, Thou Fount of Every Blessing —— 32
Count Your Blessings —— 34
Crown Him with Many Crowns —— 36

D
Down at the Cross —— 38
Doxology —— 40

F
Fairest Lord Jesus —— 42
Father, I Adore You —— 41

G

Glorify Thy Name — 50
God Will Take Care of You — 44
Grace Greater than Our Sin — 46
Great Is Thy Faithfulness — 48

H

Hallelujah, What a Savior! — 52
Have Thine Own Way, Lord — 54
He Hideth My Soul — 56
He Keeps Me Singing — 58
He Lives! — 60
He's Got the Whole World in His Hands — 62
Heaven Came Down — 64
Higher Ground — 66
His Eye Is on the Sparrow — 68
Holy, Holy, Holy! — 70
How Great Thou Art — 72

I

I Am Thine, O Lord — 74
I Have Decided to Follow Jesus — 76
I Love to Tell the Story — 78
I Love You, Lord — 51
I Need Thee Every Hour — 84
I Stand Amazed in the Presence — 80
I Surrender All — 82
I've Got Peace like a River — 85
Immortal, Invisible, God Only Wise — 86
In the Garden — 88
In the Sweet By and By — 90
It Is Well with My Soul — 92

J
Jesus, Keep Me Near the Cross --- 94
Jesus Loves Me --- 96
Jesus Paid It All --- 98
Jesus Saves! --- 100
Jesus, What a Friend for Sinners --- 102
Joyful, Joyful, We Adore Thee --- 104
Just a Closer Walk with Thee --- 106
Just As I Am --- 108

L
Leaning on the Everlasting Arms --- 110
Let Us Break Bread Together --- 112

M
My Faith Has Found a Resting Place --- 114
My Jesus, I Love Thee --- 116

N
Near to the Heart of God --- 113
No, Not One --- 118
Nothing but the Blood --- 120

O
O for a Thousand Tongues to Sing --- 122
O How He Loves You and Me --- 130
O Worship the King --- 124
Oh, How I Love Jesus --- 126
Open My Eyes, That I May See --- 128
Open Our Eyes, Lord --- 131

P
Praise Him! Praise Him! --- 132
Praise to the Lord, the Almighty --- 134

INDEX

R

Rejoice in the Lord Always ---137
Revive Us Again ---186
Rock of Ages, Cleft for Me ---138

S

Savior, Like a Shepherd Lead Us ---140
Shall We Gather at the River? ---142
Since Jesus Came into My Heart ---144
Softly and Tenderly ---146
Standing on the Promises ---148
Sweet Hour of Prayer ---150

T

Take My Hand, Precious Lord ---136
Take My Life, and Let It Be Consecrated ---152
The Old Rugged Cross ---154
The Solid Rock (My Hope Is Built) ---156
There Is a Fountain ---158
There Is Power in the Blood ---160
'Tis So Sweet to Trust in Jesus ---162
To God Be the Glory ---164
Trust and Obey ---166
Turn Your Eyes Upon Jesus ---168

V

Victory in Jesus ---170

W

We'll Understand It Better By and By ---180
Were You There? ---172
What a Friend We Have in Jesus ---174
What Wondrous Love Is This ---176
When I Survey the Wondrous Cross ---178
When the Roll Is Called Up Yonder ---182
When We All Get to Heaven ---184